# Teachin Niggas

Wesley D. Carter

Cocobarbudo Publishing, Inc.
Pennsville, NJ

ISBN-13: 978-0-578-48414-3
ISBN-10: 0-578-48414-5
Library of Congress Cataloging-in-Publication Date is available
Printed in the United States of America

Cover Artwork by Sherman Cahal

Legal Disclaimers:
While none of the stories in this book are fabricated, some of the names and details have been changed to protect the privacy of the individuals mentioned. Although the author and publisher have made every effort to ensure that the information in this book was correct at press time, the author and publisher do not assume and hereby disclaim any liability to any party for any loss, or disruption caused by errors or omissions, whether such errors or omissions result from negligence, accident, or any other cause.

The music lyrics, comedy sketch lyrics, and quotes that appear in this work are used with the intention of education, parody, and the creation of a new paradigm of thought in regards to the subject matter. Pursuant to 17 U.S. Code § 107, certain uses of copyrighted material " for purposes such as criticism, comment, news reporting, teaching, scholarship, or research, is not an infringement of copyright." The author greatly acknowledges the contributions of the artists who created the previously published material.

*For Namibia and Joaquina*

# CONTENTS

# ACKNOWLEDGEMENTS

Throughout the past decade I waited in anticipation for the use of the word *nigga* to die down among my students and on social media. I am still waiting, but maybe this book will change some minds, mouths, and fingers. I do appreciate all the support and the people who pushed me to express myself from cover to cover.

There was the late Beatrice Speir, who guided me into my first teaching job after she observed me substitute teaching, fresh out of college and the US Peace Corps. She advised me with her words, saying "the students will know if you care". Her tutelage encouraged me to show love to my students and *keep it real*.

I can't forget the late William Reed, Jr., a student who drew a picture of Che Guevara in class and let me have it in exchange for some snacks. He had the edited CD version of Cypress Hill's *Black Sunday* in class and since I thought it was promoting violence and drug use, I gave him $10 for it. I thought I was doing him a favor by not exposing his young mind to what I considered to be garbage. Little did I know that instead of throwing it away like I planned, within a few months, I would know almost all the lyrics to each of the songs. His life ended tragically the night before he was to start a job at Walmart. His smile and jovial personality still shine in my heart.

"Nothing makes a man feel better than a woman", is what Method Man rapped as he laid down a track with Mary J. Blige on *All I Need*. That's how I feel about my wife, Marisol. Thank you for putting up with me and my passive aggressiveness. You continue to be the only woman, including my late mother, daughters, and sisters, who I've never lied to. You continue to be my fantasy. I can walk through the world with a new type of freedom knowing that no other woman can eclipse your tenderness and sexuality. *Gracias.*

Ray Shakespeare, my former immediate supervisor at work, deserves many accolades and props for all his motivation. He was the only one, outside of my home to whom I revealed my book ideas. As a former teacher turned administrator, he could relate to other teachers including me, and year after year he would pester me, asking when I was finally going to write this book. Thanks for all your support during some of my darkest moments.

To my Dad, Pastor Leroy Carter, Jr.: even though this is not a Christian book, I know that you support me in my endeavors. Sorry about the profanity that appears here. The words of my mouth have been acceptable, but the meditations of my heart have been somewhat traumatized. Ever since that day after school when you told me that the n-word was wrong, I haven't used it in my spoken vocabulary. Maybe this book will convince some young fathers to teach their sons and daughters the same.

J. Story: I appreciate the time you took with me, given your super busy schedule, to hip me a bit to the writing scene. I wish you further success in the field of education and as a contemporary urban author.

None of this would be a reality if it were not for my current and former students. Read this book carefully. I am not calling all of you *niggas*. You all are of many different races, colors, and ethnicities. This book is about you if you continue to call yourself and others *niggas*. I love you like an uncle. I've always wanted what's best for you. Some of you are geniuses and you have proved that inside my classroom. You have made me a better teacher. You have given my life a purpose. I am honored to have had the opportunity to work with each and every one of you.

Last, but not least, I want to give shout outs to all my current and former coworkers - the teachers, administrators, and support staff. You are all underpaid and underappreciated in comparison to the gladiators of our times, professional athletes. Thank you for spending moments with me in the teacher's lounges; snickering with me during faculty meetings; smoking cigarettes with me in the parking lots (before I gave up tobacco over a year ago); going into the faculty bathroom behind me after my ethnic food explorations; for not rolling your eyes at me or sucking your teeth when I spoke too much Spanish; for not firing me when I couldn't turn in my IEP documents on time (my *explanation* that teaching Special Education was like having two jobs sounded like an excuse to administrators); for not complaining when I played my music too loudly in the classroom; for support-ing me and telling me that I did a good job.

# I. INTRODUCTION

I'm frustrated. We are in the new millennium and I still hear the n-word every single day. I still see the n-word in all its variations on social media every day and night. I can't keep quiet about how I feel about it any longer. I thought, maybe when the United States elected an African American president, the word would die or be killed. I was wrong. Am I airing out dirty laundry? Maybe I am, and maybe I'm not because like smoke, it truly is already in the air. However, before you think about condemning me for the title and topic, think about how some of you might not be able to comfortably tell others the title of the book you are reading. It's not my fault that we have had to hear it constantly unless we intentionally go out of our way to avoid it.

I've been teaching for over twenty-five years in an urban school district in a community that has serious socio-economic difficulties. I have taught Special Education and Spanish. I have coached baseball and chess. Yes, I spent a year or two in a suburban school to see if the grass was greener on the other side, but I returned to the city to try to make a bigger difference and continue to "give back to the community". The problems the school and community face can be complicated and simple at the same time. Most of the students I have come into contact with do not seriously see education as *the way* to get ahead. I know that this is a problem all over America right now. Too many children are learning how to become thugs, criminals, drug dealers, and junkies. After all of the struggles for civil and economic rights of the '60's and '70's, America's contemporary youth does not realize that the USA can continue to be the promised land of opportunity.

Before you judge me on the title of the book or even on my audacity for using the word in this forum, remember how many times I have to hear it stated, in one form or another, on any given weekday, within the classroom, hallway, library, or cafeteria in my brick and mortar high school. There are times when I ignore it and there are times when I don't. There are instances when I will say, "Chill out on the 'n-word'!", "Take it easy on the racial slurs!", and sometimes I might furrow my brow, smirk, suck my teeth, or shake my head. But the word has been prevalent in the language of the students I have worked with since day one of my career. It doesn't seem to be fading in popularity.

I know this sounds pessimistic and focuses on the negative, but the truth is, the bad students get the most attention these days. The low achievers are sometimes more well known by teachers and administrators than the scholars. The kid's name who punched his teacher's lights out two years ago will be well recognized when his or her name shows up on the roll this year. I was told when I was hired that if I could reach one or two, my job would be worthwhile. I thought that was crazy back then, being so narrow in scope, and I was determined to reach almost all of them. But the bad students are steadily becoming the majority and maybe my first mentor was right about only being able to seriously impact a few good ones.

Most of my students do not do homework. The majority of them come to school empty-handed and leave school the same way. In the classroom, one or two bad apples do try to spoil the bunch. It is getting increasingly hard to find good apples these days. My students have to deal with stuff that we didn't go through back in the '70's and early '80's, like AIDS, the woes of social media, music that promotes drugs, sex and violence, easy access to porn on the Internet, prevalent teenage pregnancy, and a higher level of involvement in the criminal justice system.

It's not cool to be smart in the 'hood. Nerds are shunned and bookworms get no play from the ladies. Students who do not cuss, fight, have sex, wear the latest fashions, and live out hip hop lyrics are not considered "cool". Black, Hispanic, and other mi-

11

nority kids who speak standard English are accused of "trying to be white". It's almost like they are anti-everything that teachers want them to be and no race or ethnic group is exempt.

Maybe it's an economic thing. Poor kids have come to develop their self esteem based on material things, even though this mindset leaves them in a worse money crunch. In many cases, rich parents can pave the way for their children's future and also use their economic influence to avoid problems that would otherwise sideline the dreams of an impoverished child. Many of the children I came into contact with in the more affluent school district had serious drug problems, but they seemed to be protected by the economic power and influence of their parents. They typically didn't come back after the weekend with stories of getting busted or they didn't have to visit the probation officer between classes.

Not a day has gone by in my career at the urban school when I did not hear a student say or call another student *nigga*. Sometimes, when I arrive to work, I walk to my room or to the mailbox and wait to see who will be the first one to curse or use a racial slur. It's a little game I play with myself. I want to see who's going to give me a cuss word for breakfast. Unfortunately, it may be a teacher or a security guard who is the first one to use profanity, but most likely it's a student shouting at another in the hallway or on the stairs. It might take a few minutes to hear a student call another a "nigga" or talk about "niggas", but I can almost guarantee that I will hear it before lunch.

Personally, I don't use the word. (I would be kind of embarrassed if I ever have to read this writing aloud! The word will appear here way more times than I have even thought it in my life.) Personally, I view cursing and using foul language as a sin that is somewhat easy for me to avoid. To me, cursing and using what I consider to be racial slurs have always been signs of ignorance, moral poverty, hate, and disrespect. I was raised as a preacher's kid. Foul language was strictly forbidden.

I remember cursing out loud in English a few years ago when I got bitten by a dog. The bite was a total surprise and it hurt. My mouth moved before my mind and I shouted out the word, "Motherfucker!" On another occasion, a student threw a plastic bottle at another student and it hit me instead. I am ashamed to admit that the first word that came out of my mouth was "Bitch!" It was like a primal, natural reaction. Maybe words like that one and others are resting dormant inside of me, waiting for a trigger that will ignite them in my mind like a firing pin and shoot them out through my mouth. For the great majority of my life, that trigger has had its safety engaged. Tact, respect, and conditioning from my upbringing have kept my tongue under control.

Profanity is prevalent in many parts of our society – in our spoken language, in music, movies, literature, and even in the unedited versions of television shows like *Family Guy*. We have gotten to the point where we don't even consider movies to be authentic unless the characters express themselves with some form of explicit language. However, the n-word is different. Because of this country's racist history, it has more negative connotations attached to it than other words that are considered simply as profanity.

My personal lesson about the n-word started at home. Back in the day, I came home from elementary school and in the presence of my father rhymed the word "nigger" to the lyrics to a television commercial. The ad featured Dusty, a blonde haired country girl, riding Nugget, a horse with a blonde colored mane. So instead of "Dusty, Dusty, Dusty riding Nugget, Nugget, Nugget", I sang "Dusty, Dusty, Dusty riding Nigger, Nigger, Nigger". I thought I was being creative and funny. My dad gave me a stern warning and promised a spanking if I repeated it. He was always a man of his word so I only needed to be told once! He and my mother had grown up with and survived the Civil Rights Movement, had been to Negroes-Only places, and was determined to teach his children what racial pride was all about. I immediately complied when I saw that my jokingly lyrical invention of apparent self-hate was not accepted. Ever since then, I try to control my tongue and try to be professional. (Apparently, I continue to slip up when I just so happen to be the victim of unexpected violence.) The lessons taught to me by my parents still reside and thrive within me. I still remember the threats and promises of getting my mouth washed out with soap.

When I first started working at a high school and I would hear extremely foul language coming from the students, I would say something like "Do you kiss your mother with that mouth?" or "Do you really have to use that language?" I was 24 years old, fresh out of college and the United States Peace Corps, energetic and ready to conquer the ghetto like an educational superhero. Now, I do not have the time or energy to chastise the majority of the student body. I try to focus on the students within my classroom and the lesson or paperwork I have to do. I simply give the foul mouthed students in my class a "U" on their report card, for unsatisfactory citizenship. By the way, it is still a violation of the rules to use foul language in school. It's a law that cannot be totally enforced. One principal told the teachers and staff to "choose your battles". So along those lines, I will send a student who cusses me out to the principal for disciplinary action, but the use of foul language that students direct at each other is getting so out of hand that I can't always respond to it and I shudder to think that it is becoming "normal".

It's not a coincidence that they call each other niggas. They actually have internalized the word and truly believe that they are niggas. Did they learn this at home? Do they get the idea from music? Peer pressure is still a very powerful tool, just as it was when I was a kid. But they are calling themselves *niggas* and they are acting out the meaning of the word. The word "nigger" still appears in the dictionary and there is no red line underneath it when it is typed in a word processing program. It is a legitimate word. However, *nigger* and *nigga* are not synonymous as I will describe in a minute.

The image, personality, characteristics, and the actions of being a nigga are a daily reality. I am only using the term here because it's what I constantly hear and observe. They consider themselves niggas and many are proud of it. I've battled against it for decades and now, I am still not ready to throw in the towel. I simply have to confront it. I just can't seem to ignore it.

I will continue to battle, but I feel like I am going against a modern army and I am armed with a single-shot pistol that happens to be a muzzleloader. To continue to take the narrow road of the moral high ground is what I am paid to do, and consciously, it will always be a part of me. However, as I stand facing a tsunami of immorality, I am no longer as optimistic as I was as a new teacher fresh out of college. Some teachers call in sick every now and then and call it a "mental health day". Taking a break is sometimes the only way to deal with the constant rejection that good teachers feel when attempting to instruct students who consider themselves "niggas".

To help clarify things, being a "nigga" in the new millennium is not to be confused with a racist statement. There are niggas of all colors and races. For our understanding here, students and adults qualify as niggas if they fulfill two to three or more of the following categories:

* They care very little about academics
* They have very little regard for the learning of others
* They are extremely trendy and materialistic
* They fist and gun fight over public property, neighborhood issues, and other insignificant reasons that are not worth violently risking life and limb
* They think going to jail is a normal part of life
* They get high or use drugs and complain about money problems
* Their futures are not nearly as important as the present
* They want the easy way out in almost all endeavors
* They disrespect and despise authority
* They have low self esteem
* They curse in almost every other statement and have a limited vocabulary
* They use hip hop music and lyrics in reference as to how they should live their lives
* They think sex is recreational and frequently disregard the

risks and consequences
* they are deadbeat moms and dads even if they live with their children

and most importantly:
* They call each other "nigga", "my nigg", "nick-a" or refer to females as "bitches" (when "nigga" is used to describe a male, and "bitch" is used to describe a female)

This final qualifier is the defining factor. I am sure you can argue against some of the other characteristics from the list (this is not rocket science), but students who actively refer to each other and themselves as "niggas" meet the criteria because it is a label that they self-impose and it goes deep into how they define themselves. They are the ones that we will discuss here.

  Just to clear the air, I think it's important to note that I did not work on this writing at school, on school grounds, or during school hours. I will not mention the name of the schools or districts where I have worked, although it's obvious to all who know me personally. I'm not trying to get sued or deteriorate the reputation of my workplace or coworkers. I have worked with some great teachers (some of whom taught me) and most of the time our staff members are not given the accolades that we deserve. I have also worked with some very brilliant students. They are, as Tupac Shakur put it: *roses that grew from concrete*. I am very proud to have worked with them. Any and all interviews that I have completed were done outside of school and after school hours. I don't want anyone to feel that my account was endorsed or financed by the hardworking taxpayers of our community. Writing is what I've been doing on the weekends and in my free time.

  *Teachin' Niggas* is a national challenge that compels me to share my experiences knowing very well that I am not alone. I will be the voice of so many teachers who have been unable to say what I will say here. I will bear the brunt of any criticism from people who feel I should not acknowledge the cultural phenomenon that is upon us. I am here for all the teachers who have been unable to speak because they would be accused of being racist. You have had to talk about this phenomenon behind closed doors and have had to endure in silence as you witness this astounding trend. Maybe the words that are presented here will be the catalyst for awareness and change that you have sought since your first day in the classroom.

# II. THE "N"-WORD

*Hey, I love black people, but I hate niggas, boy. Boy, I hate*
*niggas. Boy, I wish they'd let me join the Klu Klux Klan! Shit,*
*I'd do a drive-by from here to Brooklyn. I'm tired of niggas,*
*man! You can't have shit when you around niggas.*
- Chris Rock

Most of us are tired of hearing about the "N" word. It has been debated in books, on talk shows, at dinner tables, living rooms, and on street corners. "Nigger" was designed and invented by Europeans as a derivative of "Niger", an African region at the time. It was used so much as an insult, that many blacks started to use it among themselves. It became synonymous with ignorant, shiftless, lazy, and of course, African American. Over the years, especially after slavery, many blacks began to determine their own destiny by shunning the term as racist and degrading. Racist whites still used it openly until they could be punished by law or sued for its use. Blacks who had internalized the word and its identity continued to use it as instructed by the slave masters, while race-conscious blacks took on new terms like colored, Negro, black, Afro-American, and finally African American.

"Nigger" is just as American as "Kaffir" is South African. Both words were designed by European whites to verbally degrade, subjugate and patronize blacks. "We are superior, you are inferior" is what the words entail. Niggers are less than human. Sociologists and heavy thinkers feel that whites who systematically degraded blacks succeeded in creating a sense of "self-hate" that resulted in blacks feeling inferior and buying into self-degradation. Our black skin is ugly. Our kinky, natural hair is not stylish. Our lips are big. Our brains are unable to conceptualize intricate thinking and reasoning. The curves on our women are not sexy.

That's the history of the word "nigger" in a nutshell. There are other texts that dissect the word in an almost scientific way. That's not going to happen here. I will keep things simple and clear.

Today, in the new millennium, over 100 years after slavery, America still has a problem with the "N" word. Upper-class and some middle class blacks adamantly avoid using the term and will fight or sue if it is used in reference to them. Recently, the NAACP (National Association for the Advancement of Colored People) officially had a funeral for the use of the word. The late black comedian Richard Pryor swore not to use the word after becoming enlightened when he traveled to Africa. Former black football great, O.J. Simpson was acquitted of double homicide most likely because of the reasonable doubt associated with a racist cop who lied about using the word *nigger*.

The reason why conscious blacks are so concerned about the n-words' death is that they realize that there is a double standard with the words' use. When Michael Richards, a white American who played Kramer on the highly popular show Seinfeld from the '90's, got heckled and lost his cool during a stand up comedy routine and shouted out "Nigger" numerous times along with references to hanging blacks, the debate over the n-word came to a head. He was condemned and in my opinion, ruined the legacy of what was a funny and high quality sitcom. Black people who used the word had been ignored, but when whites and other races used the word, they were labeled as racist hate mongers. How can one race of people use a word in the same language and others not be able to? It was a double standard. So some conscious blacks are starting to attempt to ban the word from use by all. It is a gesture fueled by pride and heritage, but is it too late to save this generation?

I wanted the word to be dead, too, but I hear it everyday and most of the time I hear it out of the mouths of blacks and

Puerto Ricans. Whites, Asian Americans, and others say it too, when the situation is appropriate. They usually say the word either when no blacks are around or they are around a black person that they are really close to. When they are reciting rap lyrics, how can they not say the word? Comedian Dave Chappelle opened the eyes of many when he poked fun at how other races use the word and actually feel "hip" when they themselves are referred to as "niggas".

The new thing is "nigga", "niggaz", or "niggas". To an educated person, they mean almost the same as the original word, but to young people, especially fans of hip hop music, "nigga" is a new term of endearment that is synonymous to "brother", "blood", "homie", "bull", or "friend". To me, it's too close to the original word to be a new invention. But many people swear that it is new and different and that it should be distinguished from "nigger". The difference is in the pronunciation. "Nigger" stresses the "-er" at the end, that makes it an instant insult to blacks. "Nigga" has no "r" at the end and therefore makes it a word that can apply to anyone. It's crazy, I know, but we live in some crazy times.

Hip hop and rap music brought the n-word to the world. Even though it was banned from play on the radio, almost everybody got to hear the word over and over throughout the 1990's. I bought the cassette version of the album "Straight Outta Compton" in 1989 by N.W.A., Niggaz with Attitude. I couldn't resist the hard core messages and motivating beats. Eazy-E's voice, Ice Cube's lyrics, and the image of young blacks rebelling against a very brutal Los Angeles police force were contagious. Nobody wanted to hear speeches or march in a vigil with candles anymore. Even though rapper Ice-T was the first well-known L.A. gangsta rapper, (I also bought "Rhyme Pays" on LP and couldn't get enough of the song "6 in the Mornin'"), N.W.A. blew the minds of Americans, rich and poor. You couldn't buy the edited version that removed the curses and the n-word. It just didn't make sense. I still had a conscious, though. I didn't dare let my parents hear what I was listening to and I would skip over the word as I sang the lyrics aloud.

It's interesting to note, however, that many rap artists who use the word "nigga" in their songs are not actually niggas themselves. They are too smart to qualify for that label. They are opportunists who use the word to make money, but at home, they are educated and they make sure their children get the best that this country has to offer. Like Fab 5 Freddy pointed out in the b-boy breakdancing documentary film "The Freshest Kids", most rappers are simply actors. They might front or fake to create an image that sells. They know how vulnerable the youth are to their lyrics and they are true capitalists who could care less about the results of their messages.

The older generation was either for nigga music or against it. Most seemed to be against it. Black people who struggled in the apartheid American era didn't want to hear their own people saying nigger or nigga. To them, too many blacks got hung from trees to allow people to openly degrade African Americans with what they consider "self-degradation". Of course, there was money involved. Many people got rich and continue to get rich from using the word *nigga* in music. The militant revolutionary group the Black Panthers and the NAACP struggled and died so that black people would be respected as equals and sometimes even feared. Many older people who participated in the civil rights movement abhor hip hop and consider it as a self-hating tool that undermines decades of struggle.

In the classroom, hallways, and cafeterias of American schools, the n-word lives on. One author, Butch Slaughter, feels that it is a "Nigga Tragedy". He feels that niggas breed other niggas. Being a nigga does not simply mean that one considers him or herself a nigga or calls him or herself one. I contend that it has become a mentality and a lifestyle that young students and dropouts live. I assert that niggas are no longer only African Americans. Niggas are multiracial. They are negatively influenced by social media, music, movies, their parents, their friends, their enemies, and unfortunately, some of their teachers. These are the young people who cross my threshold and take their seats and positions in my classroom. I have to do my best to teach these niggas.

# III. NIGGA LANGUAGE

*You still stutter after certain questions*
*You keep in contact with certain exes*
*Do you, though, trust me, nigga, it's cool, though*
*Said that you was workin', but you're out here chasin' culo*
*And putas, chillin' poolside, livin' two lives*
*I could've did what you did to me to you a few times*

- Cardi B "Be Careful"

Niggas curse, swear, are loud, crude, and generally say things that teachers and professionals consider to be inappropriate. Sometimes they will choose when and where they say certain things, depending on how "nigga'd out" they are. Some can be selective, others are not.

I have a lesson activity that I have taught at the beginning of the school year that I call "Appropriate Language". The objective is to get students to describe when and where it is appropriate to use standard English and when and where it can be appropriate to use slang. This lesson applies to English and Spanish. I try to do this early to set expectations for the year or semester. I want students to tell me or come to an agreement of when and where they should use language that is appropriate or inappropriate. I stress to them that I am not saying that it is wrong to curse or to use the n-word, but that there is a time and place for everything.

Students usually agree that standard English and Spanish should be used on job interviews, in court, with teachers and principals, and most of them include the classroom. To them, slang is cool and appropriate when spoken with friends, in the cafeteria, on the phone and out in the streets. Depending on what kind of parents they have usually determines how they speak with them. Most have parents who will not tolerate getting cussed at, although many parents are hypocritical. They curse their kids out constantly and dare them to cuss back. As they say, the apple doesn't fall far from the tree, so parents who consider themselves as niggas usually have children who do the same.

My appropriate language lesson works well with regular students, but niggas seem to have short memories. Many educational experts believe that by letting students have a hand in setting the rules, helps them to internalize, or *own* the ideas that they come up with. They feel like *they* make the rules and are more prone to follow regulations that they create. But no good teacher is just going to give up control of the classroom and allow the students to set all of the rules. (We'll talk about nigga teachers later.) Niggas are natural rule-breakers. The school handbook says that profanity and racial slurs are prohibited. It's just writing on paper for niggas. They are gonna curse and degrade each other daily because that's what niggas do.

Many niggas curse because they have a very limited vocabulary. Others lack the skills necessary to control their emotions. Combining the two of these paints the picture for many niggas' language skills. Not many niggas will read a book or magazine that requires them to uncover the pronunciation and meaning of an unfamiliar word through the context of the selection. They are either reading information on the Internet, social media or one of those trashy urban novels. Both of these sources of reading material are supremely laced with profanity and inappropriate language. But once again, it's trendy, and niggas like to stay up on the happenings and be viewed as "cool" among their peers.

For the most part, as mentioned before, niggas like to take the easy way out. That applies to language, whether spoken or written. Let's look at an example of how a limited vocabulary combined with a foul mouth helps niggas get their points across. The phrase "fuck that shit" is an easy way to say many things. It could mean "forget about that", "I'm not interested", "I decide not to indulge", "I do not agree", "I didn't qualify for that job", etc. Depending on the tone and volume, phrases like this one can take on multi-meanings. Laziness, lack of education and habit, tradition, and habit become the basic explanation why niggas have foul mouths.

Niggas can be very creative when it comes to language. They invent new phrases and ways to say things all the time. Some authors try to cash in by writing books that are essentially dictionaries of slang words and phrases, but it's futile. By the time the book comes out, trends have changed, and niggas can be super trendy. What was cool to say last year is no longer in style. Words and phrases take on new meanings and are constantly in flux.

Recently, as my class and the rest of the building exited for a fire drill, I was intrigued at what one young female student said. Before the crowd was given the word to return to the building after our frigid stay outside, I heard a girl close by shout, "It's just too many niggas out here!" She was talking to a friend who responded in agreement with, "Uh-huh". Maybe I just take things too literally because I instinctively looked around, not at the student, but at the throng of students and staff members around in the immediate area. I saw people of all shades and of different races. It dawned on me that the student equated "nigga" with "people".

Her language is driven by her perception and her view that everybody is a nigga. To her, humans are niggas and animals are animals. What was even more crazy to me was that nobody else reacted to the loud comment. Of course, I would not expect niggas to react, because they hear and say things like this all day. But the teachers I saw close by did not even bat an eye. I didn't react by saying anything to the student, laughing, sucking my teeth, or even giving her a dirty look. My reaction was to look and see how others would take the statement. It was kind of like what Huey Newton would have deemed "reactionary".

I wondered to myself how the white staff members felt when or if they heard loudly and clearly "It's too many niggas out here!". None of the ones I saw seemed to notice the comment. It was almost like being around when someone breaks wind and you don't say anything. You try to pretend it didn't happen and hope that you don't smell the funk. It's probably somewhat traumatic when white teachers complete their first full school day after hearing the forbidden word all day. Imagine this: "Mr. Science Teacher, one of those niggas took my pencil!"

"Now, now, young lady. Please use appropriate language, OK?" the white teacher requests.

"What do you mean!" shouts the girl, "One of them niggas over there took my pencil!"

"Listen, I can't help you if you do not speak to me appropriately.", affirms the science teacher.

"OK", assures the young lady, "One of those niggas right over there took my writing utensil."

White teachers and those who are traditionally unable to say the n-word must walk a fine line when dealing with using the n-word. It is a very uncomfortable situation. Some members of the Ku Klux Klan have probably already hung up their hoods and sheets because to them, their struggle to downgrade the black race has already been accomplished. Others are probably totally enraged to find that a lot of white people now niggas too! But to know that after years of struggle by African Americans to identify the black man as an equal, worthy of pride and full-fledged citizenship, white teachers must be shocked when they find out how many young blacks have gone hook, line, and sinker into the idea of being a nigga. I doubt that it is something that is discussed in teacher training or grad school. Just like that fire drill showed me, however, people eventually get used to it, ignore it, or are able to tolerate it.

There are still some like me who can muster up enough strength and resolve each day to reprimand a student to use appropriate language, but for the most part, we have become immune or sedated by nigga language. We just chalk it up as a loss and hope that they will know how to turn it off when the situation presents itself. This is another instance when good teachers can get frustrated by the agony of defeat. If you really want to make a difference in modifying nigga language, prepare to be dead tired and stressed out by the end of each day.

# IV. BEING TARDY

*I'mma make my way to first class*
*Got to keep a blunt though, I always pass*
*Seen hunnies in the hallway pass*
*They all got class*
*So they get high grades for ass*
*Gas, got it in the bag*
*Something serious*
*Know it's gonna last nigga*
*Fuck an eighth period*
*We smoking every ounce til we permanently delirious*
*Sorry teachers, with reefer*
*I can't take this serious*

-    *Pro Era "Smoke High"*

The challenge of teachin' niggas starts the first thing in the morning. My school starts the day for students at 7:30 AM. Breakfast is offered at this time, usually lasting for 10-15 minutes. Breakfast is not an obligation, but students who arrive at 7:30 are required to go into the cafeteria unless they have special permission to go to other parts of the building. "Homeroom" is the second destination for students of the day in which they get to interact with teachers for the first time of the day. It is usually an informal gathering designed to handle taking attendance, informing students through announcements and school news, and generally a period of time to prepare students for the rest of the day. Homeroom lasts for another 10-15 minutes before the actual class starts. Most of the time, teachers are ready to teach their lessons and begin the "warm-up" activity, but face a somewhat empty classroom. But where are the students? Do I start my lesson with all the enthusiasm and hype that I would with a full class? Do I restart the lesson multiple times as more students trickle in? Or do I begin to foster lower expectations for my first period class and wind up teaching them less information?

Granted, 7:30 in the morning is too early. The business world starts at 9:00 AM, right? It's a nine to five world, but schools do not have that luxury. School districts have to start high school earlier because of busing. They can't bus older kids and elementary children simultaneously. Teachers have to be in school 10 minutes before the students, but we are motivated by money. If I am continuously late, I will lose my job. That's just the reality, and teachers know this when we decide to become educators. Not all students are late, but the majority are. The ones who are always late are usually the niggas. There are many reasons - explanations, not excuses - for their lateness.

The number one reason for nigga lateness is that they simply do not care about getting to school on time. A nigga doesn't care if they miss the introduction to the lesson or fail the class because of lateness. And best believe, niggas fail 1$^{st}$ period class because of being late. If a class is 90 minutes long or even 45 minutes long, missing a half hour is deadly to a passing grade. The only way a nigga can pass a 1$^{st}$ period class is if the class content and evaluation are set up to be worthless. If the teacher is letting a student pass who is there less than half the time, then that teacher is part of the problem. If the administration endorses and encourages passing invisible students or lowers the standards to accommodate missing students, they are also part of the problem.

When you look at a nigga's report card, I can almost guarantee that they fail or have been in danger of failing 1$^{st}$ period class. "How did you get an "F" in English, son?" The response at report card time is something like, "Oh, that was my 1$^{st}$ period class." It's an easy equation. They can't learn if they're not there. I'm always trying to stress reality on the job - the reality of the

29

world of work. I try to use real-life examples. I tell them over and over that they are gonna get fired if they do what they do if and when they get a job. Unlike the former superstar Allen Iverson, if a baller doesn't show up or perform diligently in practice, his or her performance in the game will also be sub-par.

Some niggas are late because of what they do before they get to school or what they do when they step into the building. I know some parents who drop off their kids in front of the school and after they pull off and make a left or right at the corner, their child walks away or hangs outside the building. They might go up the street to puff on a smoke or a blunt, or decide they want to go get some junk food from the store. They might wait for a late walking friend or simply hang outside the building talking. Some niggas get inside the building and wander the halls, spend too much time at the lockers, or waste time in the bathroom, eluding the security guards who may or may not be in the mood to usher them to class.

Our school has metal detectors. I am supremely grateful that we do have them because otherwise, niggas would bring guns and knives to school. The metal detectors are working symbols that say "We don't trust you niggas!" Niggas who really want to get a weapon inside are creative enough to do so, but they are not totally stupid. Only a fool would try to bring one into the front door. The detectors do cause a backlog of students, but the non-niggas know this and they adjust their arrival time to compensate for the long lines. If she knows that there will be a bumper-to-bumper traffic jam, what does a smart woman do? She will have to hit the road earlier whether it is to avoid traffic or to take a time-consuming longer route. Nobody can blame the metal detectors for causing lateness. They have been around since the early '90's and the good students who want to get to school and class on time accomplish promptness.

I know what you are thinking: school shootings have been committed for the most part by white students in the United States of America. You are correct. Urban schools have not had problems with mass shootings by African Americans and Hispanics. There have been some exceptions, but for the most part, school shootings and massacres involving guns in schools have been a suburban problem. Despite this, students and teachers in urban schools appreciate metal detectors because it helps make teachers and students feel safer. Historically, African Americans have not had a tradition of being suicidal. Again, there are exceptions. Because of our history of slavery and poverty, many black people feel that we "started from the bottom" and going back to the bottom does not warrant taking our own lives. That's how I feel about suicide and I feel the same way about intentionally committing an act that could lead to capital punishment.

The school has done almost all it can to force students to come on time. Administration has tried to do everything within its power to get young people into the building at 7:30 or earlier. Unfortunately, for the most part, they cannot turn late students away and return them to the streets. We would virtually have an empty school. This is paramount to suspension and mass suspensions bring unwanted attention and can actually present dangerous situations for students. The community and the media would be in an uproar if hundreds of students are sent back onto the streets for being late. It would be effective, however. Just like people with jobs know that they will be unemployed for not showing up on time, niggas need to know that they will not be promoted and praised for doing the same.

Once inside the building, there are so many late students on a daily basis, that there is no way to get them all into class in a timely fashion. Niggas who come to school late are not truly interested in getting to that first class on time. Teachers who close their doors at 7:30 are reprimanded for excluding students. Niggas know this and have developed a "grace period" of time that empowers them to hang out and waste time. I am in my classroom ready to start on time, but more than half the class is outside in the hallways wasting time and allowing me to get paid for nothing. Every now and then, I will venture out into the corridors and see niggas simply standing around at 7:45 AM. They are in school, but they are not in the classroom to learn and be taught.

31

Security guards and support staff cannot do much other than continuously asking students to move along and "go to class".

Sometimes during the day, administration will call a "hall sweep". This is a directive that in theory will suspend or discipline students who are in the corridors when they should actually be in class. You can beg a nigga to come to class on time, but you can't make them want to come to come to class on time. The hall sweep is usually effective in forcing the majority of students to go to class. Hall sweeps are usually performed later on in the day, usually after lunch periods. Niggas will hang in the halls as long as possible throughout the day, thinking that they are missing out on the social action, but in reality, they are missing out on some valuable knowledge. In the morning, we kind of just hope students will want to come to class. If I was rich, I would entice them to come with food or nutritional snacks. Alas, I cannot employ that method more than a couple times a month if I want to avoid being homeless.

I have had classes where there will be a knock on the door at ten minute intervals until the end of the class. (You can only imagine what chaos I would have to deal with if I left the door open.) Please remember that not all of the students are niggas, but the worse behaved ones usually are and they are frequently and chronically late. Do they seriously think that I can reintroduce the lesson, warm them up to the concepts, and re-teach continuously? It ain't feasible. I can do my best to make sure they get something out of the class, but try to imagine what an assembly line would be like if the ten workers who man the stations arrive at ten minute intervals throughout the shift. Production would be either dead or severely inefficient. That's what it's like in a classroom where niggas come when they feel like it and I have to constantly answer the door to admit the late ones who almost never come in ready and willing to learn.

Finally, some niggas will come to class with five minutes left of instructional time. These are the worst niggas we have to deal with. I ask them for a hall pass to at least verify where they have been. Sometimes, it's best that I don't know where they have been or what they've been doing. All I can do is shake my head and wonder what they will become in the future. They've missed all my antics, shenanigans, witty humor, entertaining methods, and all my best efforts to achieve the daily objectives. They have even missed me dancing to the music I play during independent practice. I do make it as fun and interesting as possible, no matter the subject or theme, but the ones who come just about when the bell rings for the end are lost and clueless.

Lateness points back to some of our qualifying nigga characteristics. They care very little about academic success. They are more interested in what is going on in the halls or in the streets than what is being presented to them in the classroom. Late niggas *are* smart enough to push the limits in getting to class to be able to say that they attended, but not smart enough to realize the long-range ramifications of missing out on knowledge and learning vital skills.

# V. HIP-HOP MUSIC

*I trample and stamp liars, like they were campfires*
*'Cuz vampires bite on my balls, and clamp pliers*
*And swing on my big thingamajig*
*So I'm bringing my nig' Proof for backup when I sing at my gig*
*Cause biters are falling head over heels*
*In love with every rhyme that I've said over reels*

- Eminem "Biterphobia"

Hip-hop music started out in the late 1970's and early '80's as party music and music that was laced with conscious black pride. Many people thought it was a fad, something that would fade away as a temporary trend. It has been around now for more than four decades. Now, however, most popular hip-hop music's lyrics and images are "gangsta" and focus on the most undesirable aspects of life: uninhibited sex, drugs, violence, and materialism.

Just the other day, a student came in and asked me if he could play a particular music artist on my computer. I asked him if it was edited and he said that it wasn't. Edited music is devoid of profanity and the all-popular n-word. Edited music sometimes replaced profanity or the n-word with a sound effect or a distortion of the word. I passed on his unedited street music, telling him "I need this job". A few periods later, another student came into the room with earphones on and shouted, "Mr. Carter! You gotta hear this new song!"

"Is it about sex, drugs, or violence?" I asked.

"No! It's good! It's hyped!"

It took me about five seconds of listening to find out that he'd lied to me. In the few moments that I listened, the rapper rapped to a fast-paced beat about having sex with multiple women.

"C'mon, man!", was my reply, "Just as I imagined. It's all about sex."

That's most hip-hop now. Even R&B, which is traditionally the romantic music genre created by African Americans is laced with profanity and n-words I remember being able to listen to rap music while my parents were around. Today, unfortunately, the music is degrading and to make matters worse, many parents listen to the same stuff as the kids.

When hip-hop and rap first came out, you didn't hear profanity. It was only on "underground" rap that came out later. Artists rhymed about partying, dancing, b-boying, having a good time, and black people's African roots. I considered myself a huge fan during that era. I would long to hear the hits on the radio in hopes of recording them to listen to the songs over and over until I knew them by heart. It was a music that we could be proud of, relate to, and to me, the rappers I liked were some of my new heroes.

That all changed at the end of the 1980's. Just as the group Public Enemy made black people feel good, militant about our rights as human beings, and uplifted, N.W.A., Niggaz With Attitudes, turned the tide and started to turn many blacks into niggas. "*A nigga named Ice Cube*" used his extremely creative writing and rhyming skills to get young black people to relate to his lifestyle and take on the persona of a nigga. Eazy-E's voice was irresistible as his lyrics were easy to recite. One thing that many people have come to realize about rap music is how it starts out with a contagious beat and then the lyrics very quickly become internalized. At first, many people just took it as music, with the freedom of speech at the helm. Eventually, it became a religion of sorts, with fans living out what they heard, wanting to emulate the rappers that they began to love.

That's how it continues to be with rapper Tupac Shakur. Dead to many since 1996, he is God to many hip hop fans. If you hang out with a true Tupac fan, it's like spending time with a fanatic who can quote 'Pac better than many Muslims can quote the Quran or Christians quoting the Bible. Tupac used the word "nigga" quite frequently in many of his songs. His voice was melodic like a thuggish musical instrument and no matter how some hate his lyrical content, 'Pac was very talented. Despite the autopsy pictures on the Internet and the police reports, some Tupac fans today believe that he is still alive. They feel that he faked his death like the Makaveli (Machiavelli) he claimed to be on one of his albums.

The fans of hip hop, aspire to imitate their artists in real life. This includes the dress, the walk, the talk, and the thought. Hip-hop has brought being a nigga to the masses. I thought about making a list of contemporary hip-hop artists who use the word *nigga* in their rhymes or who call themselves "nigga". But it would be a much, much shorter list to name the ones who don't. My heart was broken when my favorite group of the '80's, Run DMC, started to include the word "nigga" in their songs. Apparently, they must have thought that they had to become niggas or display a nigga image in order to get props and higher record sales in the rap world. In one of their songs, "Down With The King" that came out in 1993, Run DMC tried to go gangsta. Run, who calls himself Reverend Run now, referred to himself as a "nigga" and at the time, I simply lost respect for what the group had become and determined that I would rock out to their earlier material for the rest of my life.

I have also been a fan of The Black Eyed Peas. They are better known as a pop group, but recently, with the exit of their highly popular female member, the Peas have returned to their roots of hip-hop and rap in an album entitled *Masters of the Sun: Volume 1*. When I heard that they put out a new album, I immediately went to one of my favorite online stores to check it out before buying it. When that only provided me with snippets of songs, I decided to go to *Youtube* to listen and maybe watch a video of the new music. There were many songs on the album with *nigga* sprinkled into the verses, so I went back to the online store and was extremely pleased to find and purchase the edited version. I have probably listened to Masters of the Sun over a hundred times as I drive to work and fortunately, the Peas inserted sound effects instead of distortion for the n-word and the cussing. Would this project been just as good if written and recorded without the cursing and the use of the n-word? Obviously, I feel that it would be, but I feel like I am a minority within the minority.

I really don't know if it is a conspiracy or not, but it seems like now, rappers who don't cuss or use the n-word are not financially successful as hip-hop artists. Record company executives are responsible for what they put out, but technically, in this capitalist society, there's nothing wrong with selling death and degradation. Their goal is to make money - period. That's probably what prompted a group like Run DMC to "go nigga" back in the early 1990's. Personally, I think a true artist should stick to his or her roots and be themselves. If people don't buy the music or attend the concerts, musicians will starve. If people all of a sudden stood up and said, "We don't want to hear *nigga* in songs anymore!", they would stop producing it or they would have to take up new careers. *However*, the hip-hop world doesn't see it my way. "Nigga" sells and niggas sell records.

The hip-hop world sets the standard for what is *cool* and "hip" these days. New York rapper Naz, who claims to be progressive, enlightening, but uses "nigga" often in his raps, states on a recent work that "Hip-Hop is Dead". Most fans of the genre interpret this to mean that rap is losing its steam and people are no longer concerned with quality production. He is right in that sense, there are a lot of so-called *mumble rappers* out today, but hip-hop is alive and well and continues to be the number one motivating factor for the nigga identity. You'd be hard-pressed to find a self-proclaimed nigga who does not listen to hip-hop music.

One thing about hip-hop music is that its listeners learn the lyrics and commit them to memory. I used to do it and before the days of the Internet. We would sit there and rewind the tape and CD's continuously to write down the lyrics of songs. Hearing a song 100 times will also help to commit it to memory. Any walk through a public place will eventually lend you the opportunity to hear a fan "spitting" the lyrics of one of his or her favorite songs. Parents and teachers get frustrated and say stuff like, "You can memorize all those raps but you don't know your multiplication tables!" It's true. Niggas are so hypnotized by rap that they no longer are able to quote famous poets and writers. They know some of the rap songs better than they know the stories of their own lives.

Black people shouldn't get mad now when they hear whites and others reciting rap songs and saying "nigga". What are they supposed to do? If they are fans and they know the songs by heart, they can't pretend not to say the word. And there are songs where the word appears multiple times. There are songs that have "nigga" as part of the chorus. It's inevitable! That's another way to look at how hip-hop enabled young people of all races in America to become niggas. It's a word first, then it becomes a mindset. Afterwards, nigga becomes a way of life. Hip hop would not have survived and thrived if European Americans and other races of people did not become fans. You do the math.

The end product of this contagious musical culture are many of my students. It's also your students, your kids, your nieces and nephews, and your grandchildren. Hell, it might even be you. This is the mindset that they bring to the classroom. One of my friends thinks that it's not a true hobby to sit at home and watch music videos all day, but that's what many of them do. They are buying or pirating the CD's, MP3's and streaming what these artists put out and living what they see and hear from rappers. Rappers call themselves "niggas" because they either believe it or that's what they truly are. Our students listen, repeat and believe. Rap music has converted many of them into niggas.

# VI. THE COMMUNITY MIRROR

*Knick-knack, paddywhack, give a dog a bone*
*Put it on him, bet your nigga never comin' home*
*I'mma flex like a 'roid, I'm a ten, she a 'droid*
*Stupid hoe, unimportant, unattractive, unemployed*

- Cardi B "Bickenhead"

It took me a couple of years to realize that a school is the reflection of its community. If the people who send their kids to a school care about their homes, futures, and neighborhoods, usually that will translate into a good, wholesome environment for learning. Middle and upper class people send their children to school in hopes that one of two things will happen: (1) the child will grow up and continue to maintain success; or (2) the child will enhance the family's success. On the other hand, if a school is surrounded by a ghetto, or a neighborhood filled with crime, drugs, and apathy, its schools will be places of struggle and many times, failure.

What happened to the '60's and '70's, when lots of impoverished people made sure their children learned and got all the information they could in order to better themselves? What happened to people endorsing education as the way, the truth, and the light at the end of the tunnel? Can we blame everything on drugs? It certainly has destroyed the parenting skills of many people. How about blaming the end of affirmative action? Affirmative action was necessary to break down barriers for black people in the USA, but now, everybody is expected to do what singer James Brown preached by getting their foot in the door on their own.

I have to repeat myself by saying that not all of my students are niggas. Some of them come from good homes where the parents are concerned and make sure that their children do not end up as junkies, criminals, or dependents upon the welfare system. Some of them come from homes in which the term *nigga* is not used. I do feel bad for the good ones and at times some niggas do show moments of promise, but I do not teach at a boarding school. Boarding school parents have enough money to insulate their kids or to provide them with a safety net once they fall into the mentality of admiring or becoming niggas. Unfortunately, my students have to go home after school. And that's where some of the "un-learning" occurs. I repeat and reiterate stuff that seems like I am "teaching morals", but in reality, it's what good teachers see as what's necessary to prepare students for future studies or employment. When I tell students not to curse, steal, fight, to pay attention, work hard, and achieve at all costs and they just so happen to get the opposite message at home, it will take a super strong child to overcome. Niggas are not usually super strong when it comes to positive behavior and thought. They might get cussed out, stolen from, and have their ambitions snuffed out at home by their parents, guardians, and relatives. Usually, these family members have a greater influence on a student's present and future than teachers.

Multiracial niggas will be discussed shortly, but as far as niggas from well-to-do areas go, many of them have chosen to be niggas. For the most part, they haven't inherited it. It's a conscious decision to go against the grain that their parents and grandparents have attempted to establish. I feel like their state of "nigganess" is temporary. That's just my opinion. This is a newer trend and it will probably take a few more years to see how their communities are affected as more and more niggas pop up in the "good" neighborhoods.

Rich niggas might not have ghetto streets to call home, so they do what they can to make stuff happen. Eventually, a nigga will get bored in an environment where there is nothing crazy and scandalous happening. Niggas crave attention, ways to blow off steam, and other ways to make the hip-hop lyrics that pump through their veins come alive. Eddie Huang, the prominent restaurateur and author of *Fresh Off The Boat* is a good example of a successful man who spent his teenage years as the son of a self-made affluent Chinese businessman. Even though Eddie's dad was rich, the younger Huang decided that drugs, violence, and hip hop would be his vices. I do have to state that Eddie Huang, Esq.'s life has been a very sophisticated and complicated one and I am generalizing the concept of rich niggas when I refer to him. Although he probably still refers to himself as a *nigga*, he has obviously risen above the stereotypical status through education, hard work, entrepreneurship, and sheer genius.

The life of an affluent nigga is usually an amusement park ride that climbs, drops, spins and loops in the form of drug use, vandalism, going through the tunnel of the ecstasy of sex, violence, talking trash on social networks, or just hanging out. Well-to-do niggas will bump phat beats from rimmed-out whips in the suburbs, and for a time, get just as many props from their peers, feeling just as confident as a nigga from an urban housing project.

I was in a predominantly white neighborhood recently and I saw some young white guys with their pants sagging, underwear showing, and smoking weed. It was the weekend, so I am not sure if they were students, drop-outs, or what. But a big difference in well-to-do 'hoods is property values and regulations. Unlike in the ghetto, affluent communities do not have government subsidized housing, homelessness, or cops who are too busy to let niggas run things. The better the neighborhood or district, the more time police will have to solve problems. If up-and-coming niggas decide to let the mortgage go for a few months, not go to work, or party too much, they will not be living the good life in a good neighborhood for too long. The younger generation, or kids who rely on their parents for their well-being, can get away with it for as long as possible, but in the end, they will sink or swim. Being a nigga and being from a middle or upper-class family seems more like a phase that will lead to having to make a decision between continuing the nigga lifestyle or shunning it to maintain their parent's status quo.

The community surrounding my school is a poverty-stricken, urban environment. Education is not in the air of the atmosphere. You would find more weed smoke in the breeze than talk of reading, writing and arithmetic. Many of the neighborhood thugs rule the streets in a sense, and the police rule in another. Haven't they seen all of the top-rated movies where the bad guys lose and the good guys win? Apparently they haven't or actually believe that the criminals are destined for victory.

What's the buzz in a nigga's neighborhood? Sex, drugs, violence, and materialism. Teenage pregnancy is common and it leads to more poverty in most cases. AIDS and other sexually transmitted diseases are well-known, but still ignored until it's too late. Drugs are a nigga's dessert or maybe it's his or her appetizer. Anyone who has been halfway conscious since the 70's has seen what drugs have done to the country, especially in lower class minority communities. Niggas love to fight and not get paid for it. Niggas love to shoot and not get trophies and medals for accuracy. It's usually other niggas who get shot. The jails in America are full of niggas of all races and colors. Finally, niggas are materialistic and too short-sighted to see who reaps the profits from their trendy, dress-to-impress spending habits.

This is a reflection of the *community mirror* in many schools like mine. Teachers have to realize all of this when they design their lessons. It doesn't make the job easier and it's not an excuse to lower expectations, but it is better to know this and have it in the back of your mind than to ignore it. Even if you have niggas in the classroom who do not live in a ghetto, get to know where they are from and how they live before and after reaching the school grounds. It will allow you to understand what makes a nigga tick. It will allow you to design lessons that might stick.

# VII. NIGGA TEACHERS

*I felt so inspired by what my teacher said,*
*said I'd either be dead or be a reefer head.*
*I'm not sure if that's how adults should speak to kids,*
*especially when the only thing I did was speak in class.*
*I'll teach his ass*

- Jay-Z "So Ambitious"

Is it possible that some teachers are niggas as well? As comedian Steve Harvey would say, "Fuh-sho!" Once again, to qualify as a "nigga", one does not need to be black. In the case of teachers, it could be someone who is pseudo-professional; who really doesn't give a damn about what comes out of his or her mouth (when not being observed by administration or parents). A nigga teacher doesn't care whether or not their students learn, or refers to him or herself as a *nigga* or a *bitch*.

Just to give the good teachers credit, it must be noted that we do one of the most difficult and underappreciated of all jobs. Yes, we do get two months off with pay, but it is earned - believe me! All those mornings of getting up hours before the rest of the business world, grading papers all night, completing special education paperwork at home because there is no time to do it during the preparation period or lunch break, and spending extra time with needy students make July and August mental recovery time. The duties we do are exaggerated and made much more difficult when there are a bunch of niggas in the class. My school has not had any national teacher-of-the-year candidates, to my knowledge, but we do deserve more accolades than just a paycheck. Many people want to criticize instead of praise because just like a stage performer's two hour presentation, it is a lot easier to focus on mistakes than successes.

I am no expert. I'm not even an administrator - someone who is trained to weed out weak teachers. But I can talk about what I've seen, heard, and will probably continue to see in the future. Teaching is supposed to be a noble job that is sometimes looked upon negatively because of low pay in many areas and parts of the country. However, with any profession, sorry, weak, and lazy individuals fall through the cracks and somehow convince school districts to put them on the payroll. This is happening even more each year in urban school districts as the push for charter schools grows. Most charter schools can initially hire uncertified individuals and wind up with some niggas on their staff.

Here is a list of some of the characteristics of nigga teachers - let's break it down:

**No lesson plans** - Teachers who improvise everyday or most of the time are just as bad as some of their nigga students. No good teacher makes stuff up as they go along. Even the gym teacher has to take her or his work home with them sometimes, although they might get away with not having a written plan if they work for a gullible principal. My worst incidents of classroom management occurred when I first started teaching and I went in raw, without a consistent plan. A plan is like a train that can be stopped but not derailed. Beware of the teacher who flat out refuses to share their lesson plan. They are probably niggas playing the role, fronting like they are prepared. A couple of years ago, when the principal demanded that we turn in a plan a week ahead of time, the nigga teachers showed themselves. They tried to use everything including resistance, the contract (or lack of a contract) to avoid being scrutinized. You know your kid's teacher is a nigga if they wing it all the time with a phantom plan.

**Teachers Who Cannot Read Well** - In special education classes, there are reading level tests (assessments) that can determine the grade level on which each student is functioning. Granted, on a bad day or if the student has a very poor rapport with a teacher, the results may not be totally accurate. However, if the teacher cannot pronounce or recognize high school level words on an assessment that challenges students with a progressively difficult list of words, there is a problem. Fortunately for some teachers, most students give up on the grade level assessment before they reach words that some teachers themselves are not familiar with. Nigga teachers never took the time or didn't care to advance their vocabulary to qualify as "high school readers". Maybe they have downgraded to the level of their students after being around them so much, avoided advancing and enhancing their own education, or have allowed themselves to lower their expectations. One of my college buddies who taught school in South Carolina described a graduate student teacher who had problems reading and pronouncing words that had more than three syllables. He said that because the grad student was beautiful with big breasts and a booty to match, she had been allowed to advance to achieving a teaching certification. We have all heard of the stories of athletes who were pushed and passed through college because of their prowess on fields and courts. I wouldn't have believed that there were teachers in that same boat who successfully hide their lack of skills and make a mockery of supposedly hard-earned credentials. But I've seen it. Nigga teachers who cannot read well have their own strategies to hide their low skills along with defense mechanisms to shrug off the feeling of inadequacy. Personally, I feel that a good teacher never stops learning. I am not ashamed to pick up a dictionary when faced with a word that I have not mastered. I feel that by admitting my own weakness can model the desired behavior that I want students to employ. Nigga teachers do not want others to know that they are "faking the funk".

**Teachers With Alcohol on Their Breath** - Come on! The students can smell it. They know the scent and no type of breath mint, chewing gum or mouthwash can hide a night of boozing. I'm not talking about teachers who might come in smelling like liquor on

January the 2^nd. I'm referring to the ones who will make your eyes water when they close-talk you year round. We all have problems and maybe our vices, but nobody wants to entrust their child to a drunk. They could be very intelligent and have a marked command of the subject matter, but the genie in the bottle will take away from their ability to teach as well as a sober teacher. Teachin' niggas can drive some of us to drink, but not in the morning before work or late at night on a weekday. Sure, it's OK to have a glass of wine or a beer before bed, but not a six-pack, case or a shot glass competition. If their breath smells like rot gut in class, it's a clear indication that the bottle is more important than the lesson.

**Foul Mouthed Teachers** - There are quite a few teachers who curse around their students, curse at their students, and some of them even use the n-word along with their students. Need I say more? Of course, because when you as a parent go to a parent/teacher conference, you probably never hear this type of language coming out of the mouth of a trained professional. You probably have a hard time believing your own child if and when they come home and tell you how the mean, old teacher cursed them out. A teacher told me recently, "Yeah, I cuss them the f_ck out! Sh_t! That's what they understand!" Of course, I couldn't say anything except, I smiled, and said, "Naw, I don't cuss at them." Just like with my kids at home, I wouldn't say anything to them that I wouldn't want to hear back from them. I don't even tell them to "shut up". (I do say *cállate* in Spanish, because they can respond by saying *cállese*, which is the respectful way to say *shut up* in that language. English doesn't have that convenience.) Niggas don't think like this. They have weak vocabularies and feel empowered by profanity and racial slurs. Nigga teachers will say almost anything to their students if they know that the authorities are not listening. They are not pressured to have high moral standards. They are just niggas with degrees and access to a steady paycheck.

**Movie Projector Teachers** - "State Property", "Boyz in the Hood", "Brokeback Mountain", "Resident Evil", "The Purge", and "The Passion of Christ" are for entertainment purposes, right? Most of these movies are "R"-rated, violent flicks that have no place in the classroom. Nigga teachers don't think so. Nigga teachers will put on a movie just to keep the students occupied and unless there is a conscious parent or administrator who gets wind of it, they will get away with it. I show movies sometimes, but there is always a comprehension and writing activity associated. I try to get the students to visualize concepts through movies that make them think and I try to tie it in with the theme of the week or month. Nigga teachers don't engage their students with thoughtful productions. They feel the need to fire up the DVD player or punch up their *Netflix* account to get the students out of their hair, quiet them down, or simply to provide them with visual anesthesia. When they say, "Can we watch 'Love & Basketball'?", I said "Sure, after I get the copy and make multiple choice and essay questions." They sighed and sucked their teeth, but after I was through with them and the movie, they said things like "Wow! I never noticed that" or "How many sentences do we need to write a paragraph?" Nigga teachers just press "Play" and "Stop" with no engagement. Sure they might have a few laughs and bond with the students, but in the long run, the students who reach adulthood will look back and see how they got robbed and how the nigga teacher got paid for manipulating a remote control.

**Bootleg Movie Teachers** - These teachers are worse than the movie projector teachers because not only are they wasting their students' time, but they are also teaching them to break the law. We have all seen a bootleg movie, right? The picture quality is horrible, the sound is forgettable, and the feeling afterwards is that somebody just wasted $5. Despite this, nigga teachers feel like they are doing their students a favor by saving them money from going to the theater. Even though it is almost impossible to plan and execute a field trip these days, that's no excuse. Good

47

teachers would rather teach their students not to steal and break federal crimes than to brag about seeing a movie that is out in the theaters right now. Nigga teachers who show bootlegs are likely prone to breaking other rules that they have deemed "unjust" or unfair. Having a high quality pirated movie that is not typical bootleg is still wrong for the classroom. Most bootlegs are grainy and hard to decipher, especially during dark scenes, but niggas will swear that they are crystal clear.

**Angry Teachers** - There are teachers who are angry all the time. There are more and more of them each year. They are usually angry because they have to teach niggas. They get frustrated at the behavior, disrespect, and disregard for their lesson plans. They take it all too personally. They don't realize it, but they become niggas themselves by disrespecting almost all with whom they come into contact. They rarely smile and their constant bad attitude alienates students and staff members. Maybe they feel trapped, as if they cannot find a good job somewhere else. They might be too old to take a pay cut by going to a better school. They focus on dismissal time and retirement days when they can take their monthly stipend and get as far away from niggas as they possibly can. It might be too late for them when the task is over, however, as their high blood pressure, unhealthy habits and hard core bitterness turn them into candidates for an early appearance in the obituaries.

**Late Teachers** - We all struggle now and then to get to work before the rest of the world is shaved and showered. But that's what we get paid for. Teachers who are constantly late are a part of the problem. Like I mentioned before, first period class is sometimes a total loss. When I see students regularly sitting outside the door 15 minutes after the class was supposed to start, it might mean that their teacher is a nigga. If it happens once or twice a semester, that's understandable. Many teachers have families with kids and there is always some human error to take into account. But this category is for the ones who roll in "when they feel like it" almost everyday. At my school, lately the administration has been cracking down on tardy teachers. Niggas have to get themselves to work and avoid being part of the problem. Are they hung over? Did they have to have one more cigarette? No matter the excuse or explanation, the bottom line is irresponsibility. That's one of the main characteristics of niggas. They don't take too many important things seriously.

You might wonder how many of these teachers continue to fill our classrooms all over these United States. Well, there is a shortage of qualified individuals that is evidenced by the new trend of hiring international teachers who come here on work visas to teach our children. Just think of what it will be like ten years from now if the nigga mentality does not wane. Like the song says, "the children are the future", so it is only natural to see how we replenish or don't replenish our own supply of teachers. If you don't believe me, take a look at a high school yearbook from 1970. You will undoubtedly see quite a few individuals who went on to become the aging professionals of today. Now flip through the pages in the year 2018. We haven't gotten less intelligent, but we have raised a generation that is ill-prepared to fill the empty shoes.

**Teachers Who Say** *Nigga* - I have actually heard a teacher or two say to me, "Man, these niggas are crazy!" Undoubtedly, there are African American and Hispanic teachers who openly use the word *nigga* with little to no consequences. That's a double standard in the world of professional pedagogy, but it is a reality. White teachers would face extreme criticism for using the term even if it is distinguished from the racist term *nigger*. Nevertheless, I ask, how can one make it through 12 years of school, 4 years of college, and at least 2 years of graduate school and still actively use the word *nigga* in their everyday language? It's a mystery to me. I can attempt to understand it but I refuse to accept it as being professional.

Maybe that teacher is an extreme fan of hip hop and has internalized the use of the word as part of their own personal identity. They can quote all the latest rhymes, watch all the new videos, and is a hip hop connoisseur.

Perhaps that teacher feels that they can endear themselves to their students by using the word, tightening their bond with their young learners, creating a sense of being cool, hip, and up with the times.

Possibly that teacher grew up hearing the word from his or her parents, was called that in their neighborhood, and ingrained the word into their own vocabulary. However, if after 16 or more years of education they learned to avoid using the word during public speaking or at the job interview, it is obvious that their use of *nigga* is a conscious decision. To me, it's a wrong decision and that's why they fall into this category.

Eldridge Cleaver was a very controversial member of the revolutionary Black Panther Party for Self-Defense back during the Civil Rights Movement. He was no saint, and as Minister of Information he said a lot of things that Huey Newton and Bobby Seale didn't agree with, but Eldridge said "There is no more neutrality in the world. You either have to be part of the solution, or you're going to be part of the problem". This is what nigga teachers need to consider. The good news is that all of the characteristics mentioned above can be remedied by introspection to create a personal, intentional, and professional revolution.

# VIII. MULTIRACIAL NIGGAS

*Check it out ese, you're looking at the jefe, of that*
*clica with the big bad trece*
*I teach you a lesson, no question, get your ass out,*
*now you're passing out*
*When you look at the cuete*
*4 and 3 and 2 and 1, The robbery don't stop 'til I get done*
*Some niggas do this shit for fun, Now the puercos got me on the run*

-

- Cypress Hill "Locotes"

African Americans undoubtedly have the patent on being niggas. Many have internalized the original design of the nigga identity and have set the standard for what a "real nigga" is supposed to be. But we are not alone anymore. You can find nigga students of all colors and in almost all schools. They are lazy, immoral, and settle for the worst parts of the American nightmare. And yes, they do call each other "nigga". They almost always avoid calling each other "nigger", because that is an exclusive insult to blacks and is considered a racial slur by all parties involved. Because of the history of the word and how conscious blacks are sensitive to it, some other ethnic groups are careful about when and where they use the term. They don't want to be labeled "racist" and many don't want to get fired, punched or shot for insulting a hot-headed black person. But it takes more than just calling each other "nigga" to be a nigga and in the classroom, niggas can be black, white, Hispanic, Native American, Asian American, and multiracial.

Some Hispanics are special. When it comes to actual color, many of them are just as brown or dark as African Americans. In fact, a whole lot of Puerto Ricans, Cubans, and Dominicans have African blood, even though they might identify with their nationality or homeland more than they do to a color. In Puerto Rico and Cuba, slavery lasted longer than it did here in the United States. This gives them special privileges around American blacks. They get to call each other and black people "nigga" and no one even thinks twice about calling them a racist. It's interesting, because not all Hispanics have the same "permit". Mexicans, people from Central America and South American Hispanics must earn the permit to call a black a "nigga" or use the word freely. This right can be earned by spending time in the U.S., hanging around with, and becoming cool with people of color. Most immigrants from Central and South American countries do not have time to be niggas because they are too busy making the best of the American job market dream or they might not be fans of hip hop music.

There are a lot of Puerto Rican students who consider themselves to be *niggas*. When a Puerto Rican student calls another student "nigga" or uses the word in class, nobody gets upset or accuses them of racism. Even white or light-skinned Puerto Ricans have a "nigga permit". They have lived in the ghetto with blacks and have faced roaches and racism. Since they are technically not immigrants, many have grown up on welfare, public housing, and materialistic aspirations just like American blacks. In reggaeton music, invented by Puerto Ricans, the word *nigga* is often heard. It has been transformed into *Spanglish* and is not out of place in songs that might be totally rapped and sung in Spanish. For many teachers, it doesn't matter if a nigga is Puerto Rican or black. Their approach and perspective on education will be the same, in English or Spanish.

I was so surprised after I came home from the Peace Corps in Central America when I found out that Puerto Ricans have a word for "nigger" in Spanish. (Yes, you read it right - nigger - not nigga! The word in Spanish is meant for blacks as an insult.) I shouldn't have been so shocked because I bumped heads in Guatemala when I noticed that all blacks, no matter how old or how big, were called *negrito.* The "*-ito*' on the end of the word means young or small. Essentially, they think and refer to black men as "little black boys" and that's what their word literally means.

I was the only African American in a group of 70 volunteers coming from the United States and of course, I had to represent my ethnic group to the best of my ability. I can only guess that there were not many African Americans who were willing to leave the country and basically make no money doing volunteer work. Niggas want to make money, but they don't want to invest the time that can contribute to big bucks. To me, it was a once-in-a-lifetime chance to get out of the United States with a solid support network. (Thanks, President Kennedy!) My goal was to learn Spanish while helping people and I felt like I did a good job and it was a great experience. We had small classes that were held six days a week to learn Spanish. There were four students for each teacher. It was a well-designed immersion into the language and living with a host family for three months enhanced my learning, big time.

One day in class, we opened up a book and there was a picture of a young black boy holding and eating a watermelon that was bigger than him. To make things worse, the caption had something about "negrito" in it. I was pissed, but my teacher tried to tell me that they love black people and they call them *negrito* to show that love and affection. I told her "*No nací ayer*" (I wasn't born yesterday) and looked around the class pointing out the watermelon to the gringos. The other students hadn't grown up in the 1950's and '60's either, and fortunately, they agreed with me.

In that same group of 70 volunteer trainees was a guy from Texas. He was boisterous, humorous and had charisma with the rest of the volunteers. *Texas* and I both enjoyed smoking Guatemalan cigarettes and one day, between sessions of learning agricultural techniques we chatted while taking a smoke break. That day, either he or I had run out of smokes so we decided to share a cigarette. As I passed it back to him, he laughed and stated mat-ter-of-factly, "I hope you don't have nigger lips!" I looked at him bewildered and shocked and asked him what he said. He repeated, "You know, *nigger lips*. When you pass a smoke to someone and it comes back wet?" I looked at him like he was crazy and told him, bluntly, "I don't play that nigger shit!" He responded by saying that he was sorry and that his friends back home, white and black, referred to the leaving moisture on the tip of a cigarette filter as being *nigger lips*. He apologized again and I sincerely felt that he would not repeat it and needless to say, the smoke break and the camaraderie that went with it was over.

Unfortunately, that was not the end of my nigger experi-ences with Texas during our 3-month training in Guatemala. Like I said, he was charismatic, so during a trip to the frigid area of a mountainous regional city called Huehuetenango, we were all staying in a  hotel. Texas had a large group of volunteers around him, enthralled by a story he was telling. There was something about the way he was telling the story with his booming voice and southern drawl that made me want to listen and kind of raised the hairs on the back of my neck like a dog on alert. I had always been a little fearful of the American South after growing up reading about Emmett Till and the voter rights campaigns in places like Mississippi. Soon enough, even from the next room, I heard Texas using the n-word in his story. The first time I thought I heard it, I wasn't sure. I didn't want to look like the over-sen-sitive black guy, shellshocked by growing up in a racist nation, bringing that insecurity to a foreign country and essentially ruin-ing the story. I did ruin the story, however, when he repeated it, clear as a moonlit night with a floodlight.

I busted into the room, stopping the story as I threatened to kick his ass and shouted to him about how ridiculous he was, coming to a foreign country, to serve and represent our coun-try, when he couldn't even respect the people from our country. I huffed and puffed for a minute and then decided not to attack him physically. His storytelling was over for the night, though. I figured that some of the other volunteers needed me to let them know that they shouldn't have been listening to racist crap like that, but as I left them sitting there looking stunned and went out to the balcony, I just couldn't calm down. I felt myself shivering and trying to contain my anger mixed with trying to raise my body temperature. The mix was fatal to my composure as the cold, anger, and a stream of volunteers coming over to console me brought me to tears.

Texas didn't get disciplined about the incident. I didn't snitch him out to our directors. I saw him a week or so later in a warmer part of the country at the house of a veteran volunteer and we talked civilly. By that time, word had gotten around that he was getting sent back to the States for failing to become proficient in Spanish. I felt that it was a form of poetic justice. I actually hoped he had learned something from our confrontations. I even shared a joint of extremely prohibited marijuana that the small group was passing around. (Weed was a big no-no in the Peace Corps in Guatemala. We were told during our three-day training in Miami before flying to Guatemala City that even an accusation of puffing herb without proof was enough to send us home packing, with a negative evaluation.) We let our differences go up in smoke as I said a proverbial *good riddance* to Texas. I didn't feel that he deserved to represent our country and I was content knowing that he had disqualified himself through his cultural insensitivity.

I learned enough Spanish in Guatemala to be able to understand the racist mentality of some Spanish speakers and I realized this when I got back to the USA and started substitute teaching in a diverse community. Racist Puerto Ricans call African Americans *mollo, molla, molleto,* or *molleta.* When I first heard it, I thought that they were referring to blacks in general, then I found out that the word for a black Puerto Rican was *prieto* or *prieta.* I was angry when I found out that no matter how successful a black man can get, other people will invent ways to specifically keep him down. I thought a black American was just as black as a black Puerto Rican or a black Guatemalan. (The Garifuna people who mainly reside on Guatemala's Caribbean coast are black and they speak Spanish and an African-based language called Garifuna.) Of course, after I learned its meaning and discussed it with some educated Hispanics, I was convinced of its intent.

Most black people just take it for granted that there are racist people in the world. It's almost like second nature. Many of us are educated in the tenets of white supremacy. So when I would hear the words used for nigger in Spanish around school, I called them on it and they were surprised that I knew what they were saying. I started to make some progress, however, when my Puerto Rican students would apologize to me and say, "My bad, *Mala mía*" after calling a group of black girls *molletas*.

Mexican Americans niggas are usually Chicanos, those who are born in this country. They have become a part of the ghetto culture and adopt the hip-hop styles of language and behavior. Have you ever listened to the music of Cypress Hill? It's hard for them to be nice guys if many around them are in gangs, drugs, and have the screw-the-system mentality. Peer pressure can cause them to rebel against their hard working immigrant parents and grandparents who they sometimes look at as being foolish because they might not have all the material luxuries. This country would be in serious trouble had it not been for the hard-working Mexican immigrants who keep crops growing and distributed throughout the U.S.A. The old image of a lazy Mexican taking a siesta is shunned by nigga Chicano students, but they unwittingly adopt that image in their rebellion against a country that they have known all of their lives.

The former Mexican president, Vicente Fox, said that blacks in this country are too lazy to do the work that Mexican immigrants perform in the fields and in the workplace here in America. He would have been more accurate to say that niggas don't want to do the work. That would include blacks, whites, browns, and some Mexican Americans. Go to a school in Los Angeles and you will see what the truth is. Mexican American niggas are just as shiftless as all niggas. They don't have to worry about deportation, they don't always plan on sending money to Mexico, and they are definitely not going to move south of the border.

I like to watch traditional English language movies and films in Spanish when that audio option is available. Sometimes I will turn on the Spanish subtitles to read along. I do this to enhance my skills. As an instructor of Spanish it is in my best interest to learn as much as I can and be able to totally focus my mind on my craft. It would be ridiculous for a teacher to consider themselves competent, highly qualified, and an expert at what they do if they don't totally buy into and enjoy what they do.

I have issues with Spanish subtitles for English movies because many times, the translation is not accurate or it does not convey the feeling of what was said in English. This is particularly apparent when the word *nigger* or *nigga* shows up in the dialogue. It's always the same deal: *nigger* and *nigga* get translated to *negro* in Spanish. *Negro* means black. In some Spanish speaking cultures, to call someone *negro* is not an insult, it's just stating a fact. In other countries, it can be considered an insult because of the negative connotations associated with the color and/or race of black. When Malcolm X reeducated himself in prison, he saw how the word *black* has been used to describe a plethora of negative ideas. In Spanish subtitles, it's racism rearing its ugly international head. Every now and then, I will see the word *nigga* translated to *amigo* (friend) when the slang is used in a movie as a term of endearment. You can see how complicated and confusing this can become, but the intricacies of using the n-word across borders can result in misconceptions especially for the uneducated.

I was playing one of Sony Playstation's *Black Ops* renditions online with my cheap headset on late one night. I was probably one of the oldest guys playing, so as usual, I am mostly a quiet listener because there are so many young niggas on the game constantly talking trash. I am a classic "camper", a sniper or warrior who likes to hide and pick off the enemy running around out in the open. This one guy was really laying it on thick, bragging and talking about his clan and how good they were in team gamebattles. (A "clan", like in Somalia, is a gang of fighters who team together to battle other clans - not to be confused with the Klan.) I paid it no mind until he started talking about his life on a Native

American Reservation.

"Niggas be gettin' it in on my reservation!", he bragged, "I can get the best weed around because we grow it ourselves!"

My ears lit up. I was astonished to find out that there are Native Americans who consider themselves as niggas. I struck up a conversation with him and found out that he was 18 years old, and had dropped out of school on the "rez".

"Yeah, it's the ghetto here and niggas don't take no shit! It's boring as hell most of the time, so we get lit and hustle because we ain't got too many jobs to choose from."

I told him I was a teacher and he informed me that the schools there are "wack" and that he wants to move so that he can hustle weed somewhere else and maybe hook up with a white chick who will make his life easier. We both put each other on our friends list and I wished him well and preached to him a little about cleaning up his act. I was a little pessimistic because after hearing him talk with no inhibitions whatsoever, I chalked him up as a true nigga who will probably do time one day and will have a hard time reversing his destructive ways of thinking.

I know a teacher in Maryland who has students of all colors, races and creeds. She really blew my mind when she informed me that some of the Asian students are worse than the others in terms of work ethic. I had bought into the stereotype in college about hard-working, no-nonsense Asian Americans who seemed to be born with a higher intellect and a better grasp on technology, mathematics, and science. I quickly realized that it was not their genetics, but their culture that hones and shapes them for academic success. I hardly ever saw Asian students partying with us at the University of Pennsylvania. I figured that they were engineering students who would sooner fall on a sword before bringing home a "C". The Maryland teacher says that that's bull crap. There are Asian niggas too!

In the movie "The Hot Chick" starring Rob Schneider, the Asian mother who owns a nail salon in the mall is humorously portrayed as a "ghetto hoochie" who pimp walks with fat gold chains, and drives a lowrider with hydraulics. When her daughter shuns her as being an embarrassment, she responds with the classic dis' of "Nigga please!" My daughters and I have seen this movie countless times and we always laugh when we see this part because she says it with an accent and it seems so out of place to see an older Asian call someone a "nigga". However, similar to the Mexicans, many of the young Asian Americans who are born in this country do not have the same ideals as their parents and many have bought in to what we know as hip hop culture.

The owners of one of the Korean stores in my city have daughters who used to work with them in the business. I particularly remember one of them who was in her early twenties at the time and was definitely a beauty queen. I've only had a crush on two Asian women in my life that I've met in person. One went to Penn and I would see her occasionally on the elevator in High Rise North during my junior year. She never even cracked a smile when I would speak to her. The other was this hottie at the Ma-Pa Store in my neighborhood. She probably showed me more love behind the bulletproof counter's plexiglass than her parents wanted her to. I rarely go into that store anymore, but I do recall that after a couple of conversations with her, she didn't come around too much anymore. She straight-up disappeared. I think her parents were protecting her from me and from the other blacks and Latinos who make up the bulk of their customers. But it just goes to show how the younger generation of Asians are not so interested anymore in following in their parents' progressive, but restrictive footsteps. Many are becoming niggas in the way they see the world and it can show in the classroom.

Granted, the teacher in Maryland teaches in a somewhat affluent school district. But like I mentioned before, being rich does not exempt one from becoming a nigga. Being well-to-do may help to reform the nigga that rears its ugly head in young Asians. The teacher told me that some of the Asian students are lazy, violent, and perform poorly academically. She didn't go so far as to call them "niggas", but that's what I am here for: to interpret the characteristics of niggas regardless of what the typical notion of a nigga is to people who stereotype.

Last, but definitely not least are the white niggas. European American niggas have become so numerous, that some fools made up a nickname for them: *wiggas*. I try to steer clear of racial stereotypes, but teachers hear them all and sometimes they do become more than just trends. White niggas in this country might outnumber black ones simply due to sheer numbers in population. The white teachers that I've talked to are embarrassed, but admit that in the new millennium, there are thousands and thousands of white nigga students.

White niggas exhibit all the characteristics of other nigga students with one exception: they can have an easier time shedding the nigga persona or assimilating back into productive society. Most people believe that the large numbers of white nigga students originated from rebellion motivated by drugs, hip hop, and peer pressure. Maybe it's just how our capitalistic society is designed - few hold money, power, and respect, while the masses are downtrodden strugglers. White niggas are becoming a part of the masses, selfishly looking out for the individual, but not quite interested in progress of others.

I just watched the movie "Havoc", a drama about rich suburban white kids who are into gangs, drugs, sex, and hip hop. It's an older movie, from 2005, but well worth the time to watch. The movie is a very good visual example of white niggas. They call each other "wiggas" and "niggas" and think it's cool to act "ghetto" in the streets and in school despite their affluent lives at home. There are some real white niggas shown in the movie, but most are wannabe's, who get a thrill out of living life on the edge and getting to rub shoulders with true thugs from the 'hood.

Just as ridiculous as it is for blacks to accuse other upwardly mobile blacks of "trying to be white", white niggas are accused of trying to be black. They are seen as "posers" or copycats looking for an identity. Hip hop supports this notion. Most people who buy hip hop CD's, download and stream the music are young whites. Hip hop artists are predominantly black and the fans often shun white rappers unless they are extremely talented like Eminem or other award-winners.

Why do I keep referring to hip hop? It's because of how people internalize the lyrics. I was the same way, especially in 1989 when I repeatedly listened to LL Cool J's album "Walking With a Panther". I wanted to do everything LL was rhyming about as well as dress like him, talk like him, and essentially, *be him*. For hip hop heads, it can be a religion. So, it's not strange to think that many whites who exhibit nigga ways are hard core hip hop fans. It is a consuming music genre that alters and forms the way people act and think.

As we can see, it's not just blacks and Puerto Ricans who call each other "nigga" here in the good ole U.S. of A. In a classroom full of kids who cuss, come to class high on drugs, ignore the efforts of the educators, vape in the bathrooms, and who refuse to study at home, color, ethnicity, and race do not matter as much. A nigga can be a nigga regardless of whether or not they were taught the word by their parents or grandparents. It's also the way some students act, visualize themselves, treat others, and treat themselves that qualify them as "niggas". More than likely, they do utilize the word daily. Many teachers wonder if they will grow out of it, but most of us see very little light at the end of the tunnel.

# IX. NIGGAS IN THE SYSTEM

*Where's my niggaz? On the lock-down*
*Damn, I'm locked up, they won't let me out*

- Akon "Locked Up"

A couple of weeks ago in class, I tried to get the lesson started, but it didn't quite go the way I had planned. You have to realize that as a teacher who tries to relate with the students, I often find myself talking to them about everything that they want to talk about. Sometimes it is better to spend a few minutes talking through one of their topics instead of having to deal with the topic sporadically throughout the class period. For teens and young adults, it is easier to talk to a teacher (that will keep their information confidential) than it is to discuss some of these same issues with their parents. Even though I do not consider myself as one of my students' friends, I do sometimes consider myself as like an uncle - someone they can talk to - who probably won't respond with the explosive emotions of a parent. If I do not accomplish the lesson, I can at least feel satisfaction that they are learning, expressing themselves, and hopefully using appropriate language. We started on the subject of incarceration and the legal system. Most of the students in my small class that day had been arrested and locked up at least once in their young lives. One had on an ankle monitor, some are on probation or undergo regular drug testing and they have hundreds of stories to tell.

Public Enemy called jail "an anti-nigga machine". I interpreted their rap as explaining how jail is against niggas and is a systematic way of keeping them from becoming successful inside and afterwards on the outside. What the song and the students I've talked to fail to recognize is *why* they were locked up in the first place. There are a few innocent people in jail, but most of them are as guilty as sin and unfortunately, will continue in their evil ways in the future.

I almost always find out when one of my students has been locked up. If it does not appear in the local newspaper, the students will tell me before the day is over. I also am a "roamer" in my classroom. I walk around and I will jump into the student's conversations if I feel the need. Maybe I'm nosy, but that's just one of the ways I get up close and personal. Long gone are the days when a teacher sits behind his or her desk and hopes to manage a classroom from a safe distance. Proximity and a keen ear helps me to prevent the niggas from starting fights, dealing drugs, gambling, or any other preventable plot that is brewing.

There are days when I just do not have the energy to roam and be constantly interactive. Teaching in a public high school usually means larger class sizes and multiple levels of ability within one classroom. Translation: energy drain! I have to stay hyped, stay in shape, stay alert, and never be totally inert. But who knows? The extra energy that I put into my students can make a difference in whether or not they decide to become a con. Committing crime *is* usually a conscious decision.

Getting arrested is no big deal for most niggas. It's almost like a right of passage that gives them the needed reputation and common experience among their peers. When a student gets locked up on a Friday and shows up to school on Monday, the other students and the teacher don't rush up to them, hug them, hold them, asking, "Are you OK?" "Did they hurt you in there?" or "I am so glad that you are home!" Nope, these days a trip to the slammer for a nigga is no big deal. It's like getting suspended from the streets just like they get suspended from school.

They have so many people who have also been locked up that they can relate to. Once a student asked me in disbelief saying, "What?! Mr. Carter, you've never been locked up before?" I told him that if I had been locked up, I wouldn't be able to be a teacher. (Which is not totally true, but somewhat accurate in most states depending on the offense.) So many of their fathers, uncles, aunts, brothers, sisters, and mothers have been locked up that it gives them the sense that incarceration is inevitable and normal. Niggas do not like cops and probably hate judges. Hip-hop music artists are niggas' idols and they rap about getting locked up and most of them have been locked up. They emulate hip hop artists in this regard. Most get jailed for drugs, violence or stealing. To a nigga, these become legitimate reasons why they should go ahead and get themselves locked up too.

One of my former students who didn't make it to graduation considered himself a nigga, but in my perspective, was very talented and eclectic. He delved into realms that most of the other students didn't bother to contemplate. He was into listening to multiple genres of music. He discussed the concept of anarchy. He was a multilingual skateboarder, a ladies man, and a graffiti artist. He bragged about sexing up a female student on the school's roof and his ability to access unauthorized parts of the building were unheralded.

Unfortunately, a year or so after he was supposed to graduate, he found himself behind bars for a serious crime. According to a local newspaper, my former student accidentally killed his baby son. His biggest mistake was not calling 9-1-1 after the incident and he was sentenced to 4-9 years in jail. The story stated that he was afraid that if he called the police, he would be accused of child abuse and never be able to be the father that he wanted to be. I was in disbelief and it hurt me emotionally, but it was hard to ignore the factual details of his case. After he was sentenced, placed, and eventually transferred to a local jail, I decided to write him.

We exchanged a steady stream of letters. He never asked me for anything monetary. He sent me the last pictures that he had of his lost son and I made sure his sister got them. I started to notice something incredible and depressing about the letters he sent. He would garnish the envelopes with artwork. I was in awe of his skill and detail. Some students have considered me to be artistic and have complimented me on some of the ways I can manipulate chalk and pencils, but this former student was obviously a master of the craft. His skills reminded me of West Indian Archie, a real-life character in the former criminal life of Malcolm X. Archie was a mathematician, but because of how his life had been molded by society during the apartheid era of America, he relegated himself to running lottery numbers. Malcolm lamented on how Archie could have been a great scientist, engineer, or mathematician if society had dealt him a fair hand.

My incarcerated former student had talent that the world needed to see and appreciate. I would post some of his work on social networks, give him credit, and implore the cyber world to *free him*. We became genuine pen pals and I looked forward to seeing his new creations. I purchased and sent him the novel *Dirty Havana Trilogy*, by the Cuban author Pedro Juan Gutierrez. It's a gritty collection of short stories that defined the real Cuba of the 1990's for me. When my former student wrote me back a few weeks later, he told me that he had read the book 11 times, from cover to cover. Why couldn't I get him to read so much as a fraction of that in my classes? Why did getting locked down have to be the means to inspire his world-class art skills?

Teachers like me want to save niggas right here and now. We want to convert them and get them to reject the label, the lifestyle, and the inner feelings with which they define themselves. We try not to live with regrets about students who wind up in the system because our efforts are continuous and genuine. We try to learn to live with failures, telling ourselves *well, at least we tried.* We lead the proverbial horses to water and implore them to drink. We struggle to convince them to want better for themselves. We wish we could download inner dreams and desires into their brains and hearts and delete the files in their minds that whisper to them that going to jail is no big deal.

Self-esteem is low among most niggas, so fighting happens on a regular basis. It's usually he-say, she-say gossip, or over a girlfriend or boyfriend. It can also be gang-related or one of the neighborhood vs. neighborhood wars that spill into the school. Niggas get really excited about fights. They want to talk about them and give a descriptive play-by-play account. When students ask me if I saw the fight, I will say something like, "What, the Mayweather - Pacquiao fight?" They might laugh, but they are talking about a school fight that happens in the hallway, classroom or cafeteria. Just like in prison, fighting gives them a reputation that makes the winner feel good about him or herself. Some fighters are immediately arrested and taken to the police station for processing. Unless there are aggravating factors like weapons or serious injuries, most niggas who fight will either be back in school a few days later or they will get sent to an alternative school for a month or so.

Niggas are impulsive and enjoy the moment. As with drugs and fighting, niggas will indulge in the moment and not regard the long-term effects. Drugs lead to addiction, which can lead to either unemployment, poverty, jail, or death from overdose. Fighting can do the same thing, but increasingly, it can lead to a violent death. Many niggas cannot take a loss in a fist fight without retaliating later to save face. The retaliation usually includes guns. Looking at the big picture, a small disagreement can cost a life.

I spent the majority of a school day a few years ago mourning when one of my 1st period students was shot and killed as he walked to school. He never made it to class after being shot and collapsing a couple blocks away from the school. I was crushed at the idea that his short life was ended because his 'hood had beef with another. One of my female students came in late that morning and said that she heard that her classmate had been shot. I was hoping it wasn't true, but I had to do something. I immediately looked up his mother's phone number, called her, and she answered. I asked her to call his cell phone because another student said he might be involved in some "street drama". I didn't mention the exact nature of the rumor that I heard. I didn't feel that would have been appropriate. She thanked me for calling and we hung up.

Our school was put on lockdown shortly thereafter. I tried to remain calm and hoped that like the rapper 50 Cent, who had been shot 9 times and survived, my young, football playing student would also be able to recover and maybe even continue his efforts in the classroom and on the gridiron. When the word came through that he didn't make it I sent all my students to the math classroom next door to me. Fortunately, the Algebra teacher understood and helped me out by accommodating them. I didn't want to be around anybody that day. I didn't want my students to see me crying. Nigga or not, my young bull didn't deserve to die. I didn't want to hear anybody's jokes or laughter, even if they would be totally unrelated to the tragedy at hand. Just because my fallen student lived in a neighborhood he had been associated with their drama.

In silence, and between wiping my tears, I chalked a huge mural of his name on a board in the classroom that eventually would be signed by hundreds of students, photographed, and untouched until my classroom was relocated the following school year. I looked for him on social media. I like to avoid having my current students as friends on social media to maintain a productive teacher-student relationship, but I hoped to find him and see his face and eyes clearly through my tears. I found pictures of him professing his love for John Madden football video games. I found pictures of him sitting in our school's classrooms. I found one picture that I didn't want to see. My student, with a couple other guys, pointing their index and middle fingers held together towards the camera with their other hands cupped underneath their hands. To me, in my mind at the time, this was the picture that got him killed. To me, this was the gangster photo; the nigga pic. Between teardrops falling on the tiled floor of my lonely classroom, I wished that he hadn't taken that photo or even was forced or coerced to live that life.

Sadly, and frustratingly, my former 1st period Spanish student's killer has never faced justice. My student was killed in the broad cold-blooded daylight of a morning in May or June. The unwritten law that niggas adhere to is *no snitching*. Even though a few students have told me that they know who killed him, "snitches get stitches" or worse. The philosophy and practice mirrors what goes on in jail. Even though his killer could have been another student within our school, I didn't want to know who he was. I didn't want them to tell me his name. Knowing my conscience, how I feel about my students, and my own personal concept of justice, my knowledge of who the killer is could lead to more violence and death. Think about it. If I know, I'm going to want to tell the authorities. They will want the person who told me to testify and that would put a bullseye on the back of the "snitcher". *Coño*, that would make me a target too.

Fortunately, within the walls of the school building, teachers are not considered to be snitches. We see a student do something against the rules, and depending on how we want to handle the situation, we act upon it. That's not snitching. That's enforcing the rules and teaching young people how to act and conform to the norms of our school community. I can't think of a situation inside a school in which I felt afraid to "rat out" a student. There have been times when I have picked my battles, but I have never feared retaliation for sending a student to the principal for doing something I didn't think I had the authority to handle. Although prison guards and wardens are often responsible for enforcing violations of the rules, they are not considered to be snitches either. They are simply doing their jobs and attempting to get the inmates to adhere to the rules. The parallels of teachers to correctional officers are strikingly similar especially in situations in which niggas force teachers to push learning into the background.

Violence can be virtually incvitable in many cases. Niggas run the block. Niggas control the 'hood when the police are not around, and what are young men and women supposed to do about that? I wouldn't want to stay in the house all day and night trying to avoid the negative elements of the *barrio*. Eventually, one has to walk to a car, walk to the store, walk to the bus stop, or walk to school. What kind of life is that? To live under siege is

not living in my opinion, so unfortunately, young people - especially niggas - feel compelled to collectively represent and defend
the neighborhoods where they live. In the frame of mind of Jay Z,
DMX, Memphis Bleek, and Beenie Sigel, neighborhoods compete
with each other for money, cash and hoes. In more professional
terms, finances, respect, and available relationship partners are
often the elements that define what a neighborhood values and
are willing to die for. Unfortunately, as we noted earlier, the
school is a reflection of the community, and inevitably, the violent mentality becomes a part of the school environment.

Schools like mine are wise to have metal detectors and
occasional police officers within the building. Also, there is a
security force of a few safety personnel, or guards, who are essentially unarmed police with arresting powers. Throughout my
career, I have seen different methods of control employed by security force members, including using walkie talkies, physical
restraint, harsh language, and pepper spray. Some liberal minded
folks would argue that having cops, metal detectors, cameras and
the like create an environment similar to that of a jail. They feel
that treating the students with love and freedom will encourage
them to act appropriately, effectively raising their self-esteem
and expectations. These kind hearted methods are no good for
niggas. Niggas test the limits and push the envelope just to satisfy
their own hunger for attention, violence, recognition, and street
reputation.

For a nigga, the school is the safest place to fight. They are
almost guaranteed that they will not get shot during the fight.
If they are getting handled, pounded on, or losing the fight, they
can usually count on the fight being broken up and stopped by
security or by a physically confident teacher. I have broken up
about ten fights during my career. The last time I broke up a fight,
there was no security around so the other Spanish teacher and
myself decided (without consulting each other) to break up the
fight ourselves. We both came to our doors after hearing a profan-
ity-laced commotion outside our classrooms. The other teacher
is younger than me, so I instinctively went to grab the student

who looked like he was losing, while my counterpart restrained the student who was punishing his opponent the most. I'm not sure if you can understand this in words, but when I grabbed the so-called loser around his waist and pulled him backwards away from the slugger, I felt no resistance. I felt what seemed to me to be his body giving out a sigh of relief.

The "loser" somehow lost a sneaker during the fight and the punisher grabbed it after we separated the two and threw it down a long flight of stairs, adding pain to punishment, putting a final stamp on his victory. My Spanish-teaching counterpart was saying, "Don't throw his sneaker!", but the punisher shouted "Fuck him and his sneaker!" while tossing it. Afterwards, when all the drama was over and security had showed up to escort the students away, the other Spanish teacher and I went back to our doors and shared a chuckle when I stated ¡Eso fue fácil! ("That was easy!") During other fights that I had broken up throughout the years, it had never been so easy. Almost every time I broke up a fight, I wound up injuring myself - usually a finger or a hand. Once, I banged my head on the lockers and bled while restraining a student who along with another were jumping a kid.

In the streets, who can they rely on to make sure they are not killed during a fight? Police response time is erratic, especially if the loser is banking on someone calling the cops. So many people today record fights with their cell phones and seldom if ever do we see the cameraman or camerawoman put down the cell phone to stop a fight or intervene. Schools like mine also have cameras that can verify self-defense or involvement in a fight if charges are pressed. It is unfortunate, but fighting in school can almost be considered a wise decision if the strategy is to have an old fashioned, fair fist fight.

The thing that intrigues me is how even though getting arrested, locked up, and having a criminal record is clearly one of the worst things that can happen to a young person, assault and aggravated assault continue to be common practices. As with tattoos, I constantly preach to my students about waiting until they are older and have a career to make permanent decisions. Tattoos can eliminate a candidate for a job depending on the nature of the job or the location of the tattoo. Criminal records are red flags for employers too, and can determine the economic fate of a young person for the rest of their working lives. Juvenile records are not considered or viewed after reaching adulthood unless they involve a felony, giving a kid a chance to begin their adult life with a fresh perspective. Unfortunately, too many niggas decide to continue in crime even as they become adults. They think that they are smarter or sneakier than the authorities and that usually leads to bigger crimes that warrant bigger time.

For the most part, the students who I have come into contact with have serious criminal records because of drugs or violence. Niggas want to get high or make quick money selling weed, coke, crack or meth. Sometimes when I am driving down the street, I see young guys rolling up blunts or "dutchies" in broad daylight. I have always taught in states in which marijuana has not been legal and it is definitely not legal or authorized for use by minors. Last year, I saw one of my students rolling up a blunt of marijuana in the middle of the street. He was literally in the middle of the street. He was walking, twisting, and licking while standing on the double yellow lines! After that, I'll admit I teased him about it. I started calling him "the Dutch Master". I think that if there really was a "war on drugs", the cops would have an easy time catching most of the users in cities like mine. Unfortunately, the Dutch Master and other niggas like him have very limited recreational activities in the ghetto. Getting locked up for drugs has become a very common problem all over the country and obviously, users get less time and punishment than do the dealers.

As more states move to legalize marijuana, perhaps we will see less of our young people ending up behind bars. Niggas are going to get high, no matter the laws or the cost and weed is the drug of choice for most hip-hop heads. The harder, more chemical drugs will always present a deadly problem in this country and in this world. However, the perception that niggas have about jail is a big part of the problem. Incarceration as a right of passage must end in the mentality of our youth. Quite frankly, niggas shouldn't feel that they have to go to jail to become men and women.

# X. PART-TIME JOB NIGGAS

*Nigga, I was tryin' to get it on my own,*
*Working all night, traffic on the way home*

- Drake "Started From The Bottom"

Another frustrating aspect of teaching niggas is knowing what many will face in the world of work. The very nature of considering oneself "a nigga" will almost guarantee closed doors, glass ceilings and sandy floors in the working world. Because most niggas cannot turn their negative behaviors on and off for extended periods of time, say eight hours a day or forty hours a week, most will face hard times contributing to society. Many will fail to be successful in employment and financially for some of the same reasons why they perform poorly in school.

The main reasons why high school niggas don't get and keep good jobs is for absences and lateness. You will fail if you don't come to class and you will not get paid for not showing up to work. Getting to work late is just like arriving tardy to class. You missed out on this and that and you will have to catch up, stay later, try to get others to cover for you, or eventually get fired because you couldn't or weren't willing to do what you had to do to accomplish what you missed. "No-call, No-show" can be like a nigga's middle name. Work is just like school except the pay is grades and on a job it's money. Both can lead to even more money in the future.

Teachers are taught not to mix discipline with academics. This means that if a student is a terror in the classroom, you can't give her a bad grade because of how she acts. In reality, terrorizing kids get bad grades because they are too busy being a disturbance to learn the knowledge that it takes to get good grades. Let's call that *poetic injustice*. Niggas who get bad grades because of poor behavior usually wind up unable to get or keep a good job because of the same reasons.

My high school students have probably heard me say a thousand times that "you won't be able to keep a job doing that". It's true. Niggas can't curse out their bosses and get away with it more than once or twice. Break things on purpose or vandalize the workplace and a nigga should expect a pink slip. Skip work and hang outside on the very grounds of the job site and see what happens. Sleep on the job and dream about the next one, minus a good reference from the present gig. Flat out refuse to work today and watch what your check will look like. Come to work high on marijuana, smelling like weed and the job will be gone faster than the buzz.

Many niggas go to work at fast food restaurants because they offer entry level jobs that require little to no skill and frequently have openings. Once they get the job, they can learn how to prepare food, package it, count money, make change, and perform customer service. My second job ever was at Kentucky Fried Chicken as a cook. I learned how to fold back the wing tips and fry chicken, but I hated it. I stayed long enough to be able to afford my first used car. For unskilled workers, fast food joints are sometimes the only available places of employment. As society and the "new world order" sends so many jobs overseas to save money and to turn a hefty profit, unskilled people have to either get educated or skilled to become middle to upper class, or remain in the lower class at service jobs.

Back in the day, a person with a high school diploma could get a good job, feed a family, buy a house, and even buy a new car. That can happen today, but most niggas don't think it's cool to make the sacrifices necessary to compete in today's world market. Sometimes they are too busy trying to look and feel rich *now* without working hard for it. I surprised my students recently when I told them that no matter what name-brand shoes, boots and sneakers they have on, most if not all were made in China or Southeast Asia. We even looked inside our shirt collars to see where they were made. I told them that the next time they "burn on", or criticize, another student for having a not-so-popular brand name, to remember that they are all reppin' Chinese boots and sneakers. They needed to know that the good paying, low-skilled jobs that they once could get are no longer around. They have to get educated or skilled to make it in the new millennium.

I don't mean to degrade fast food restaurants because per-sonally, I can't live without them. I love the burgers, fish sand-wiches, onion rings, fries, and drinks that can be purchased from my car after speaking into a microphone. When I worked at KFC, I didn't like it, but I took pride in my job. It was hard work with tough hours. The chicken had to be prepared right every time in a regimented way to insure quality and good taste. Stealing was not allowed and not necessary because we were allowed to take home all the leftover chicken that we wanted. It was a good ex-perience, but it also taught me that I didn't want to make a living in an entry level job that had no benefits. I am sure the managers made good money, but unfortunately, most niggas don't get that far.

An old girlfriend of mine worked in a Taco Bell and would come home with interesting stories about the niggas who worked there. She didn't refer to them as "niggas", but I could put two and two together. Tales of sex, drugs, saliva, indifference, and stealing would make our late night conversations interesting. She made me afraid to go to the restaurant to eat late at night be-cause apparently, that's when the worst, most unreliable niggas manned the shift.

I have always been turned off by fast food niggas who curse loudly while preparing my food or while waiting on me in line. I can understand a slip-up here and there, but blatant, loud and in-different cussin' is not good for customer satisfaction. In one fast food restaurant, I actually said, "C'mon lady, I don't want you cus-sin' on my food!" (Fortunately, she was ashamed and didn't cuss me out!) My dad raised me to not be afraid to voice my opinion, but I learned later in life to have a filter and to pick my battles. To me, if culinary artists don't care about being presentable to customers or themselves, they will not care about what they want me to chew and swallow. Thank goodness for surveillance cameras and those extreme video television shows that expose so many people who spit into and do worse to people's food before serving it! This seems to help in quality control, and give good people the hope that maybe workers will prefer to keep their jobs rather than have me eat a piece of their fecal matter or their semen inside a sesame seed bun.

Fast food can be a stepping stone for a nigga: an eye opener perhaps that will introduce them to legal money making, socializing with others, feeling self-esteem about maintaining a steady job. That could mean conversion from *nigga* to *regular person*; from *nigga to man or woman*. That is a beautiful thing. They definitely can feel like they are contributing to society because there have been days that I've eaten fast food for breakfast, lunch, and dinner. (Except Chick-Fil-A on a Sunday!) I try to convince students to stay on the job for at least six months so that they will have a presentable reputation for their resume, job application, and to provide future employers with the assurance that they are not fly-by-night employees. Also, it's a lot easier finding a new job while you have a job. Fast food helps to avoid that feeling of total hopelessness that can many times lead to a life of crime.

# XI. DRUG NIGGAS

*Soon as the bell rings, I got a song to sing*
*I got future plans of smugglin' grams and keys*
*I missed my first class, my thoughts flooded with visions of cash*
*And my rivalries, intentions to mash*
*With these goofy ass hoes*
*Goofy ass MC's and goofy ass flows*
*Wannabe G's, how you gon' roam like you hard?*
*You in my zone nigga, I own the school yard*

-    *Tha Dogg Pound "School Yard"*

Weed and hallucinogenic drugs became popular in the late 1960's. The seventies continued with marijuana and heroin. The '80's was the cocaine decade. Powder turned to rock and the fiends didn't stop in the '90's. Now in the new millennium, all of the above drugs are still around with methamphetamines, pills and ecstasy as popular alternatives. Of course I am generalizing, but niggas today are overwhelmingly into drugs.

The United States has to be the number one drug-using country in the world. This writing is not all about statistics and technical talk (not that I'm too lazy to look them up, I just want to keep things simple), but it's obvious that Americans are getting high everyday and all day. Almost everyone of us knows someone who has wasted most of their life getting high, "zooted", blasted, or cracked out. If not, you have seen it on the news. Watch a few episodes of *Cops* or stream *Narcos* and see how people of all races, ages, creeds, and colors dedicate their lives to chasing the feeling of a drug. We have to include alcohol, because it can just as dangerous if not more, than some of the illegal drugs.

I am starting to sound like a scratched CD or a buffering stream when mentioning hip hop music as the catalyst for many nigga habits, but the music does support the drug game. I have heard Ja Rule and 50 Cent rap about taking ecstasy. Hundreds of rappers rap about getting high smoking weed. You will even hear crack and meth mentioned here and there, but the number one topic in rap as it relates to hard drugs is selling it.

Some of my students, who consider themselves niggas, talk openly about drugs. When I was in high school, drugs and cocaine dealing were just starting to become popular, but no matter what crazy stuff we were into, we didn't want the teacher to know about it. We talked among ourselves, out of the listening range of teachers and adults. Niggas today have very little discretion. By the end of the day, I can tell you which students are on drugs, who is sleeping with who, and what they are gonna be doing with their money tonight.

At the beginning of my career, teachers were encouraged to refer students with drug problems to counseling so that they could be rehabilitated. As the years went on the system got overloaded, social workers and assistants found their positions cut because of funding problems and now the concern is more geared towards apprehending students who bring drugs to school or who attempt to sell drugs on school property.

When students talk about drugs in class, I try to change the subject or refocus them to what we are supposed to be learning. However, other times, I will listen and encourage them to get or stay clean. They can't think of any good jobs that do not drug test and neither can I. I would rather talk to them about drugs and the dangers associated with them than try to shut them up and alienate them from discussing it with someone like me who can redirect their thinking. For many students, the teacher who listens might be the only sensible adult they get to converse with on a daily basis.

Niggas drink too, at early ages. They know more about hard liquor than I do. I'm a fuzzy navel, mojito, Mai Tai type of guy. I'm a lightweight. Whatever seems to be popularly mentioned in rap songs seems to be something that they've tried or drink when the situation presents itself in their lives outside of school. In R&B songs, alcoholic beverages are a prerequisite to making love. Sometimes, the alcohol that these underage niggas drink is given to them by parents or family members. Other times, they find ways to buy it or get someone else to get them a taste. It's a peer pride thing to get drunk. "I'm getting drunk on Christmas, ya'll," shouted one of my female students. "Me too, I'm gonna get fucked up!" replied another.

I can't relate to their excitement. When I drank a whole bottle of orange Mad Dog 20/20 alone in my dorm one night at Penn, it was a life shattering moment. Some people referred to Mad Dog and another drink called Sisqo as "liquid crack". I drank a bottle by myself and it tasted good. By the time I looked, there was less than an inch left in the tall, rectangular, thick glass container. That was when the room started spinning and all of a sudden, deep inside my head I heard a voice boom, "Lay down!" I complied, but that didn't stop the room from twisting around me. As I closed my eyes to stop the spinning, I prayed and asked the Lord to let me see the next day alive. I promised Him that if He did, I would never touch Mad Dog again. When I miraculously woke up the next morning, I was relieved and happy. I have not touched liquid crack ever since. I'm too scared!

The attraction of selling drugs seems to have many niggas in a constant trance. Hardworking adults see it as "easy money". It ain't easy, but we still know and believe that it's not a respectable way of living. It's not even a smart way of living because there is no security, very little longevity, it's very dangerous, and it's very destructive to family, society, and life. Niggas don't care about that. They see money. They see fast money that can be made within their community. It's that right now materialism that drives niggas to participate in the drug economy in order to get things that would take you and I years to attain.

There is no end in sight to the so-called "War on Drugs". The government is not going to legalize hard drugs. People don't seem to be getting tired of getting high. Niggas are still aspiring to be drug kingpins and queens. The jails are getting filled with drug offenders, big and small. Teachers can't stop preaching, though. The message is getting through to some. I can still feel confident that some of my students do not use drugs.

The best time to catch drug-minded niggas in a classroom is before they get high or after the high wears off. Sobriety mixes well with learning. When a stoned student comes in smelling of tobacco laced weed, I tell them that they can't get a good job on drugs, try to blow their high by preaching a little to them, and then I hand them a spray bottle of cologne that I keep on my desk. We are instructed to send students who we suspect of being under the influence of drugs to the nurse. I've been down that road and the majority of students who I have sent or referred to the nurse usually decide to exit stage left, avoiding the nurse and avoiding her examination. I sometimes think of a particular student who I referred to the nurse years ago. I'm not going to sugar coat how things transpired. I'll just tell you about what happened.

He considered himself a nigga. He always used that term when describing himself and others, while using the word *bitch* in reference to a female. I sent him to the nurse because he reeked of cheap weed, "reggie", as it is called, for being *regular* in quality. He did the darndest thing. He actually went to the nurse. It was determined that he was under the influence of marijuana, was referred for counseling, got in trouble with his parents and from that moment on, his life spiralled in a downward trajectory. When I saw him on the street years later, his life was still in a shambles. He never completed school, never held a job for more than a couple months, and was unable to support the children he had fathered. Man, did I feel guilty! Why didn't I just hand him some cologne or one of those vials of Muslim oil that I kept in my desk to hide the cigarette smell from my own fingers and clothes after my lunch breaks?

Sometimes doing the right thing sucks! It was hard not to blame myself for doing what I have been instructed to do. I have to convince myself that I can't save them all. Niggas are gonna do what niggas want to do. But now I am a bit shell-shocked. If a nigga walks by the security guards as they enter the building in the morning reeking like that, then my battle has already been picked for me. Conversely, in the case of reporting suspected child abuse, that's a whole different story. That is a battle that I will always involve myself in no matter the outcome. But for the Pepe Le Pew niggas who come to my class, I have cologne for you...and a half-hearted pass to the nurse.

What's going to happen now that marijuana is becoming legal in many states of our Union? My state has legalized medical marijuana and on a recent lunch break during an in-service day, I chatted with two teachers who managed to finagle themselves some medical marijuana cards. Secretly, I was envious. I have always had a soft spot for that good green. I don't endorse or promote it for kids, but over the years I have indulged on quite a few occasions. I can flat out say that I have never gone to work high. My eyes get too red after smoking weed and my students are not dumb. Niggas are not dumb either, especially the ones that get high on weed. They would spot my eyes from a hallway away. I would compromise everything I stand for if I showed up to work high. Plus, I would be so nervous about getting caught that it wouldn't be worth the effort.

It's been a long time since I've smoked marijuana and as Katt Williams said, "I've got the papers to prove it!" Weed and teaching don't mix. Weed and studying don't mix well either so it's fortunate that under legalization it will be regulated. Will students smoke more once it is totally legal? We shall find out, but my guess is that there won't be an extreme rush by our young people to go grab a bag. I haven't seen any articles or news reports from legal states in which there is an outcry over a new wave of pothead students. Those who smoke it now with no plans to quit will keep on puffing.

I want my students to know that there is a feeling of invincibility when they have a clean body and a weed-free system. Clean urine opens up many doors. Right now, if I want to get a part-time job working at Amazon for $15/hour, and there are positions available, I can do it. If I want to drive commercially and make dollars for every mile I cruise, I am just an application away. Niggas might feel more allegiance towards the lyrics of the hottest hip hop track from their favorite smoked-out rapper, but I want them to pledge allegiance to opportunity. Just because weed is steadily becoming more and more legal throughout the United States and the world, good jobs will continue to require their workers to have clear minds and clean urine.

# XII. THE NIGGA PROM

*I'mma a hard stun'n nigga like Evil Knievel*
*Jumpin' out Lex's and Hummers - showin' off for my people*
*I'm the # 1 stunna!*
*Wh-what, wh-what, what?*
*The # 1 stunna!*
*Wh-what, wh-what, what?*

- Big Tymers "#1 Stunna"

Niggas love to stunt and "floss", live for the moment, and let the world know that they are having a good time. There is no better time like the prom to be classy and flashy. Proms and formals for all ages are applicable, but the big deal is the Senior Prom.

The senior prom is a time when niggas go all out for one night of extravagance. No one should knock the prom for what it is - a final chance to culminate the high school experience in a formal celebration. All students should go to their prom. It's a once-in-a-lifetime experience. But niggas can take it too far these days. To them, it seems that prom night is planned to be the last night on earth. Some spend thousands of dollars or their parents go into serious debt to go out with a big bang.

Traditionally, as in my case as a high school senior, a young man rents a tuxedo and gets his date a nice bouquet of flowers. Also, he rents a car or makes sure the car he has or borrows is washed and detailed. The young lady has a dress made or buys one, gets shoes, gets beautified with makeup and has her hair and nails done. A few couples may make provisions and pool their money to rent a limousine. They all have a good time, they dance, they eat, maybe fool around afterwards, and get home later than ever.

Twerking is off the hook! Niggas love to twerk. (If you don't know what twerking is, search it up. I'm laughing for you and at you for not knowing about it!) A lot of the dancing that niggas do these days is basically having sex with clothes on and twerking is no exception. I specifically remember a comment that a prom photographer made about last year's prom festivities. He said it got so hot and sweaty in the ballroom and on the dance floor that it smelled like "ass and fish". I laughed while turning up my nose when he told me the gory details of all the twerking that went on. "But, they had fun though!"

Niggas turn the prom into a major investment. So much of a nigga's self esteem is attached to materialism that the prom is a do or die chance to be the biggest, best, or most beautiful. Many adults do something similar. They spend ten thousand dollars to get married and after the lavish honeymoon, they return home to their rented apartment. Afterwards, when the euphoria wears off, they sometimes begin the spiral towards the break up.

For most of my career, I have worked with low-income students. It has been amazing and disheartening to see copious amounts of money that are spent on the senior prom considering the limited resources of the partygoers' families. Hundreds and thousands of dollars are spent for one night. There is no regard for next month's bills or any other future investment. The same thing happens with cell phone bills. Cell phones have become a major investment for families struggling to shake off generational poverty. This is the *nigga* way of thinking - "live for today". That also means spend for today.

Because college might not be an option or a thought, blowing the bank account is worth it, right? She looks so fine, so elegant, so much better than the rest. He's flossing like a movie star, driving a brand new luxury vehicle, nobody can touch him. Together, they are stunning; the world is theirs for one night. If drugs and alcohol are involved after the dance, the couple will take their trip across the universe.

It's not easy to *hate on* the prom because it is such a fun and memorable event. I went to two senior proms and I enjoyed both of them immensely. The thing is, I didn't go broke for the prom. I had enough money left over to be ready for what came after the formal celebration. I didn't have to ask my parents for money because I worked to earn enough to look good and feel good. The prom is no time to be cheap, but niggas have turned it into a spending competition.

There's the prom with the horse and carriage. There's the Rolls Royce with the color coded suit to match the exterior of the car and the dress that matches the plush interior. There's the outrageous jewelry. I have even heard of prom dates showing up in a chartered helicopter. Niggas love this. Teachers hate to see hardworking families spend their last and more to show off and try to upstage one another. We do want to see the kids have a good time. We want to see them focusing on bright, academic and vocational futures. We don't want them to be niggas, especially on prom night.

# XIII. GRADUATION

*Cool is how I played the tenth grade*
*I thought it was all about macking hoes and wearing pimp fade*
*Instead of being in class, I'd rather be up in some ass*
*Not, thinking about them six courses that I need to pass*
*Graduation rolled around like rolly-pollies*
*Damn, that's fucked up I should've listened when my mama told me*
*That, if you play now, you gonna suffer later*
*Figured she was talking yang yang, so I paid her no attention*

- OutKast "Git Up, Get Out"

The truth is, many niggas do not graduate. In American cities, especially the larger ones, there is a high drop-out rate. It gets even worse for minorities like blacks and Latinos, when you look at the statistics. Getting through 12 years of school can be too much for a nigga to handle. There are so many pitfalls that it isn't really funny. For the ones that do graduate, getting a diploma is a genuinely positive step in the lives of niggas.

Unfortunately, many niggas graduate simply because the schools can no longer afford to have them around. "Get them outta here", is what many teachers and administrators think, with a sigh of relief and a dim hope that the next batch will be more manageable or more willing to learn. Some teachers feel like holding a student back does them no good even if they can't properly fill out a job application. "Pass them on."

Putting students up to "their right grade" is a concept that grew in the 1990's and it became known to me as "social promotion". I remember an episode from the television animated series "The Simpsons" in which Bart, the young male cartoon character (who acts like a nigga in many ways), was retained in his present grade until he was academically ready to be promoted. (I considered Bart's character a nigga even though the networks can't afford to take the risk of agreeing with my opinion. He meets almost all of the criteria except he doesn't use the n-word.) Time lapses in the episode and the next thing you know, you have an old man sitting in a middle school.

Of course, the age limit in most states for high school students is around 19 for regular education. Special education students can go to school until they are 21. Most of them don't take advantage of this, obviously. Special ed niggas want to get out of school and be done with books just as badly as regular ed kids.

As the time nears for graduation, niggas turn in poorly conceived term papers, cheat on tests, beg, plead, and try to bribe their way out so they can "walk". Parents who have never met their children's teachers come out of the woodwork to lobby and complain in order to change failing grades into "D's" and "C's". Graduation is still a very big deal, as family members finally show up at an official function to see their young offspring get the ticket they need in order to move on to bigger and better things. That's all a diploma is nowadays. For a nigga, it doesn't represent 12 years of hard work, learning, cultural exploration, enlightenment and achievement. It's just a ticket or a stub that says, "Yeah, I went to that school".

The graduation is a gala event. The biggest part about graduation night is not the pomp and circumstance or the keynote speaker. It's not even the photo shoot of the diploma handout that is now characterized by repeated requests that the parents refrain from being disruptive when their child's name is called. The most hyped part of the night happens during what I will call the "blast-by" (not to be confused with drive-by shootings). It is a requirement, or a ritual of driving around town, honking the horn, hanging out of sunroofs and windows, putting everybody on blast that the niggas just graduated.

The blasts of horns, shouting, and all that stuff can go on for hours. It is usually followed by partying, alcohol, drugs and sex. (Maybe not in that order, but all are usually included). Remember that most niggas live for today and go all out. The blast-by is fun for non-nigga students too, right? But when it is over, the non-niggas have other things to do. They might dabble a little in the festivities, but they are not going to blow their money on partying like there is no tomorrow. Niggas will "party like it's 1999", because for many, life will continue to be one long party after graduation night ends.

Teachers want their students to know that achieving a high school diploma is very important, but it is only the beginning in the lives of the new post-graduates. In the new world economy, with some exceptions, a high school diploma is not sufficient for gaining a career that will enable a young person to become a major contributor to society. Not all students go on to attend college, but for the majority of graduates, teachers desire to see them attend post-secondary educational or vocational institutions, including the military. The challenge in teachin' niggas is to convince them to set goals *before* they begin high school. Those goals do not have to be specific. Not many of us knew we would become teachers when we were 13 and 14 years old. However, if that seed of achievement is planted into the minds of middle schoolers, they will take high school and the precious transcript that runs from 9th to 12th grade much more seriously. When that happens, the symbolic turning of the tassel will take on a new meaning. It would signify a launch instead of a landing.

# XIV. NIGGA FEEDBACK

*Our niggers are better than their niggers*
-     *President Richard Nixon*

I had been trying to write this while keeping it away from my wife and kids. I really didn't want them to walk in on me and see what I was working on. But any married man who has a wife who cares and is even slightly jealous or cautious about her man cannot get away with constant typing on a computer without their better half getting suspicious and wondering what's going on. She might think that I'm having an affair, chatting, or communicating with women on a social network or on one of those personal community websites.

She walked in again last night and said, "What are you doing?"

"Working on a book."

I guess she was tired of that redundant response and came closer, saying, "Let me see."

I couldn't stop her, so she looks at the screen and I'm sure that the first thing she saw was the word "nigga" multiple times with the red underline. The spell check's red underline is just like a highlighter.

I looked up at her, cocked my head to the side, smiled and shrugged my shoulders, trying to use body language to justify what I was writing.

"Ooh, Baby. You can't write that! How can you call your students *niggers*?"

"I am not calling them *niggers*, it's *niggas*", I replied. "And that's what they call themselves. Not all of them, just the ones that call each other that."

"Well, that's most of them, right?" she asked.

"Yeah. I'm tired of denying it. You know I don't like the term, and you don't hear me saying the word, but I hear it so many times every day that I just feel like giving up and letting them be what they wanna be."

"People are not gonna like this book. You are gonna get in trouble."

What could I say to that? I can imagine some black people getting mad at me if they don't read it or maybe I will have to find a new job. People might not see my need for therapy and writing has been therapeutic. I did tell her that I am not using real names and I don't even name the school or district where I teach. So I simply smiled and shrugged again. I wanted her to know that writing this is helping me to avoid stress and that maybe someone will benefit from reading it. She has been with me almost every evening and night after coming home from dealing with niggas.

We both struggle to keep our own kids from becoming niggas, too. Our kids know that they are going to get the same response that my father gave to me when I came home and said *nigger* as a kid. It is in our children's best interest to make sure neither my wife nor I hear anything that we consider to be profanity coming out of their mouths. My wife and I both grew up with the "spare the rod, spoil the child" philosophy.

I responded by saying, "Well, the truth hurts sometimes. Maybe the book will help them look in the mirror and they will change what they see and what they say."

And I wonder how many niggas will actually read a book that is not about new urban fiction including a sexy stripper or a drug dealer. In this age of advanced technology, reading is usually on the low-end of young people's priority lists. Reading text messages and meme captions are some of the only ways many students build their vocabulary in their spare time. I won't be able to use this text in class either. But, I understand completely. Well, at least I can hope that some teachers will be curious and pick it up to take a look.

One of my former students, is attending a four-year university and is also one of my friends on a social network. I asked her a few questions about *niggas* and she had some interesting things to say. When I sent a message asking her the meaning of "nigga", she replied:

*The word "nigga" is a word that the majority of blacks use amongst each other and towards each other. It has a variety of meanings and it all depends on the situation it is used and the tone of voice you use with it. It can be used in a friendly tone. ("Wassup my nigga?") or hostile ("What you say nigga...I'll f- you up!"). If I see two people fighting in a predominantly white neighborhood, I would say look at those "niggas"! You know, because of them being ignorant and ghetto.*

To her, niggas are essentially and typically black or African American. The word *nigga* has become a natural part of being black in America. She concludes that whites who act like *niggas* basically become niggas through their actions, but the word still applies mostly to black people.

I wanted to ask some people if they considered themselves *niggas*. I knew that the results would be kind of skewed because the obvious answer is a defensive "no". It reminds me of Laurence Fishburne's interview in the movie "Deep Cover". I enjoy that film immensely, but it is the opening job promotion interview that grabs me the most. Fishburne's character is asked by a white man, "What's the difference between a black man and a nigger?" The black cop answers point blank, "The nigger's the one who would answer that question."

When I asked my former student if she considered herself a nigga, she answered in a very interesting way:

*I don't consider myself a "nigga" but I will allow my friends to call me a nigga without complaining. So I guess I do consider myself a nigga in a certain way. But it's only when we joke around.*

So she can be a nigga when dealing with her close peers, but reserves the right to be respected when things get serious. Apparently, she doesn't consider herself to be a nigga in the eyes of anyone who is not a friend.

Like I mentioned previously, I did not write or work on any of this at work or during any school activities. Thank goodness for a twenty-four hour, seven-day-a-week world wide web. I also live in the community where I teach and get to see students in the streets. Another online friend, a former male student, graduated a few years ago. He is also attending a four-year college and during his senior year in high school was one of the best readers in school. He had this to say about being a nigga:

*I wouldn't necessarily call myself a "nigga" because of the "lazy" connotation to it, but in conversation, I have no problem if someone (who usually uses the word nigga) calls me by that name. The usual use of nigga is very important because if you're just using it exclusively for me, then I feel you are using the word under a different definition.*

He doesn't mind if someone who usually uses the word in conversations refers to him in that way, but if someone who hardly ever says the word directs it at him, it could be taken as an insult or a mistake.

I was intrigued by his response to whether or not all niggas are black. He responded:

*No, all niggas are not black (by definition). The definition doesn't has a color attached. But since those who revived the word happen to live in an all-black community and given the obvious remnants of the word nigger, give it an all-black feel. I would definitely feel indifferent to call someone white a nigga because: 1) they wouldn't understand it ("Why is he calling me a nigga?"); and 2) they don't know the definition in the way I used the word.*

Obviously, this former student has read history. A nigga today can be of any race, but he would not feel comfortable directing the term at a white person. He goes on to educate me, stating:

*Also, I read an interesting article the other day, which took the etymology of the word nigga all the way from the Egyptian word "Negher" which means God! Ain't that crazy?!*

Yes, it's definitely crazy and so interesting. I do not profess to have all of the answers, but the quest for answers is essential to our future. One of my mantras is: *a good teacher never stops learning.*

I've hoped that the use of the word has been a trend, but in one form or another, the term has been in existence for as long as this country has existed - even longer! When people wore big white t-shirts in the '90's, I waited for that to play out and like most clothing fashions and trends, it did. Wearing dress shoes without socks will eventually be a thing of the past too, but using the term *nigga* is transcending the status of being a trend. Only time will tell of what its next transformation or mutation will be.

I challenge you to ask yourself if you are a nigga. Are your parents niggas? Do your friends consider themselves niggas? Would you marry a nigga? Would you hire a nigga? Would you want a nigga to be your next president? Can niggas go to heaven? Can niggas be trusted? Would you give your life for a nigga? That's your homework!

# XV. OBAMA'S NIGGAS

*Yeah, but on the positive side*
*I think Obama provides hope and challenges minds*
*Of all races and colors to erase the hate*
*And try to love one another, so many political snakes*
*We in need of a break, I'm thinking I can trust this brother*
*But will he keep it way real?*
*Every innocent nigga in jail gets out on appeal*
*When he wins, will he really care still?*
*I feel*

- *Nas "Black President"*

It was the night of November 4, 2008. I sat in my living room all alone and wept as I watched the live feed on the television. What some people said would never happen, happened. My grandparents would have probably laughed at me and called me a fool if back in the day I said that one day a black man would become president. But it happened. It finally became a reality. A black man, an African American, a negro, a colored man was elected President of the United States of America. I was proud. I felt that I was a part of history. Years ago, comedians joked back in the day that if a black man was elected president he would probably be assassinated before he could even think about taking office. He would have to give his acceptance speech bobbing and weaving, staying on the move to avoid a sniper's bullet. But Barack Obama survived to serve two consecutive terms as the leader of our great nation. I was almost sure that as a part of this miracle of acceptance and enlightenment, the n-word had seen its last days as a staple of American vernacular. I was wrong.

Barack Obama is no nigga. To some people whose hearts are filled with racist hate he is a nigger. However, to the humane minded, clear hearted people of this nation, Obama is simply a man. He is intelligent, eloquent, graceful, and worthy of the votes that ushered him into office two times despite the competition, haters, naysayers, and racist citizens who were determined to keep a non-white man or woman out of the White House.

To me, Obama represented many things and one of them was that as our President he would help eradicate the daily use of the n-word from the mouths of America's youth. I figured that would happen especially among the African American youth. We now had someone to be proud of, to look up to, and to emulate. I thought to myself, "Can we stop calling each other niggas and bitches?" My answer was the mantra of the Obama campaign: "Yes we can!" But we couldn't. We wouldn't. And to some people, we shouldn't.

I traveled to Cuba multiple times during the time of the Obama administration, chasing tail and improving my Spanish after my first marriage disintegrated. I would drive all the way to Canada and fly down there, getting seriously interrogated the first couple of times by the Cuban authorities and welcomed routinely after they realized I wasn't a counterrevolutionary. Raul Castro was the President of that proud island nation at the time. His brother Fidel was still running things behind the scenes and publicly congratulated Barack Obama on his victory. My friends in Guantanamo told me they celebrated with rum and tobacco when Obama was elected. They too realized the historical significance of his election despite having virtually no access to the Internet and a state controlled press. I asked them when they would get a black president and they laughed at me wholeheartedly. After they stopped laughing, which was a very long time, my girlfriend's father say *nunca*, and he changed the subject.

I felt that Obama would be very influential in the black community and that his professionalism and charisma would even convince some of the more racist elements in the country to reconsider their philosophies. He had an uphill battle on all accounts. For black people, many expected him to initiate policies that would directly and positively improve their lives. For Hispanic people, many wanted him to make changes in our immigration policies to improve their families' ability to legitimize their status in this country and to facilitate the path to citizenship for those who were seeking documentation. Obama's presence alone would boost self esteem among many minorities and for many white Americans, he would represent forgiveness for the racial atrocities committed by their ancestors in this country.

I just wanted a few things from President Obama. Some were concrete and others were abstract. Of course, I wanted him to normalize relations with Cuba and end the senseless trade embargo. I felt that the embargo was actually having the opposite effect of its objectives: I felt that the blockade was sustaining the Castros, giving them a clear and present enemy to rally against. I also wanted some form of reparations for African Americans - a pipe dream, I know - but what black person would turn down a fat check to pay for the free labor of our ancestors? Most of all, I wanted something abstract. A simple statement or a speech. Obama gave the absolute greatest speeches. He was eloquent and had an impeccable memory without using notes. I wanted Barack Obama to tell black people and all people to stop using the word *nigga*.

He had to be appalled by its use himself. In 2015, he did actually use the word *nigger* in an interview. A week before, a racist white man killed several black people in a church, shooting them with no mercy or remorse. Obama explained that America had not been cured of racism and just because people aren't actually using the word *nigger* in public didn't mean that racism had been eradicated. He was addressing white on black racism and all of its forms, particularly in violence perpetrated against African Americans and how despite much progress over the years, hatred in the form of racism continues to be a hindrance to progress and peace in America.

I wanted Obama to address *niggas*. I wished he would have actually and literally said, "Stop calling each other *niggas* and *bitches*". I wanted him to address black people in particular and in effect people of all races who consider themselves to be niggas. Even if nothing became of it, I wanted to see and hear it happen. In my overly optimistic mind, I figured, "What the hell? Give it a shot!" It takes me back to my mentor, the former director of Bilingual Services at my school district who told me that if I could positively influence one student, I would have done my job. If Obama would have said "Stop calling each other niggas" and explained why it was detrimental to our self esteem, image, and our ability to view each other as fellow Americans, I was sure that a few people would have listened and taken heed.

No one is perfect, but as President, many people deified Barack Obama. If he had spoke out against using the term *nigga*, *niggaz*, or *my nig*, I would have been able to add one more item to my anti-nigga repertois. I could have referred to our beloved (or hated) president to further justify why I felt that their language and mentality were not productive or upwardly mobile. I could have told my students that calling themselves niggas and adopting the mentality of a nigga was something that would hurt their present and their future. "It's time for change" was another popular slogan associated with Barack Obama's presidency. Many students and young people could relate to Obama. They could not relate to George Bush and most do not choose to relate to Donald Trump. Many rappers mentioned Obama in their songs. I dreamed that if he told everybody to stop calling each other niggas, maybe some of the rappers and R&B singers would have decided that they could remove those words from their lyrics too.

Niggas continued to be niggas under the Obama administration. Rappers continued to rap and rhyme the word *nigga* in their songs. As a matter of fact, the word *nigga* seemed to flourish among Latinos, specifically Puerto Ricans, Dominicans, and Cubans during the Obama years. I continued to hear it everyday at work and in the streets. I knew it was too much too ask to have the President address such a controversial issue that didn't involve foreign policy, gay rights, health care, or the constant losing battle against spiteful members of his domestic enemies, the Republican Party. It was a part of my own little war; a battle against what I considered to be self-degradation among the precious minds in my classroom.

# XVI. TIPS FOR TEACHERS

*Teacher, teacher, the foe waits outside*
*To turn your children into tools for his pride*
*He's always scratchin' for a way to come in*
*Here comes a pressure group, he's tryin' again*
*Teacher, teacher, you know you're alone*
*You're boss won't save your skin; he's saving his own*
*Nor will the parents help; they'll only condemn*
*They want their children taught to be just like them*

Leslie Fish "Teacher, Teacher"

Well, now I feel a lot better. I have gotten a lot off of my chest and have spoken my mind. I still don't feel comfortable using the n-word and probably never will. It's a whole lot easier typing it than saying it! But until I am fired, retire, or take on a new career, I will come into contact with more niggas in the classroom. Will I feel better now that I have exhaled? I still cringe inside when I hear the word and see the actions of the word personified. So what do I do? What should other teachers do?

**Tip One - Don't give up!**
Hey, you've heard this one. Inspirational books, mentors, coworkers, and people who show you support will repeat this mantra of perseverance to you. No matter how bad niggas make you feel in the classroom, hold onto hope. Hold onto the hope that the young man or woman who is raising hell in your classroom can become a productive member of society. Hold onto the hope that they might raise their children to do better than they have. Be optimistic and care about who you are teaching.

Your vibe of positivism can alter a child's or young adult's future. It's better to believe this in your heart and allow hope to show through your work than to be a pessimistic ambassador of demise. Remember, you may be the only ray of hope that a nigga sees each day. You might be the only representative of normalcy that they get to be associated with each day.

**Tip Two - Be a Good Listener**

In a class of 20 or more students, chances are you don't have much time for chit-chat. If you can capture everyone's attention and hold that stance, you are blessed, entertaining, or very talented. But remember, learning is a dialogue these days. Dictator teachers are a thing of the past. To be really effective, a teacher must be a good listener as well as a talker. Niggas have issues in their lives that are important to them and if a teacher immediately waves them off as being insignificant, she will lose her connection to them.

Niggas are naturally anti-establishment in many ways, but to have someone from that establishment listen to them can break down the barrier and help to build a relationship that facilitates learning. Be an aunt or uncle in the classroom - the adult who loves them but who does not explode emotionally when they relate something personal or intimate with you. Remember, you might be the only positive person that they get to talk to all day. Many niggas are belittled each day and to have an adult show genuine interest in their lives can be instrumental to future victories.

**Tip Three - Show That You Care**

The woman who was most influential in getting my teaching career started ran a bilingual education program. She told me that the students will know if you truly care about them or not. I never forgot what she said and I still feel that it is true. I knew that by "caring" she included how I would treat them, how hard I would work for them, and how I would focus on their futures.

Caring is something that a paycheck can enhance, but not replace. Most teachers do not choose the profession because of the salary. Good teachers teach because they want to positively influence minds and consequently, lives. It's not enough money for someone who considers the action of teaching as a chore that is unbearably difficult and stressful. Loving or liking teaching is complimented by a salary because the money enables you to do something that you dreamed of or enjoy on a full stomach.

Allow that enthusiasm and drive to translate into caring for students. It does not and should not be physical, except for a handshake and an occasional hug, but it can be felt or seen in smiles, laughter and positive body language. Many niggas spend their free time with adults and individuals who are not accustomed to showing positive feelings and love. A sane man who smiles most of the time and shows happiness is not always common out on the streets. These can be seen as weaknesses in their communities. You can be a light to their darkness. And if you are just faking it through the pay periods, teaching might not be for you. Remember, niggas might not be the best in academics or even interested in academics, but they can see through the veil of a fake teacher's facade.

**Tip Four - Show Interest in Their Lives**

I like to find out what the students are interested in to manipulate these ideas later and convert them into lessons and learning experiences. As much as possible without compromising your own personality, get to know what their interests are and their aspirations. Believe me, the topics that they are interested in can be transformed into learning activities. Depending on the flexibility of your lesson plans and curricula, utilize their interests for instructional ideas. Even though I am not into hip-hop like I used to be, I take a little time to find out what's going on. I watch the news and stay informed about sports and video games. Otherwise, we can be totally out of touch with them.

Finding out what their interests are can give us clues on their learning styles. Unless a nigga is asleep, high on drugs, or has headphones on, his or her brain is still capable of taking on new knowledge. Oftentimes, getting that new knowledge into their heads is done by connecting it to some of the old and present thoughts that can be unlocked through discovering who your niggas really are. You will not always find their areas of interest on a state or normalized test, but you have a much better chance of getting your students to exhibit the desired outcomes on that exam if you gain their trust, admiration, and respect by becoming a positive part of their lives before the test. They will want to perform well for you if you have put in the effort to make learning more interesting to them.

**Tip Five - Come Each Day With a Fresh Perspective**
You see the student who cursed you out and called you a "punk ass bitch" yesterday after lunch. Immediately, in your mind, you are thinking, "This motherfucker…" Do you see him? Yes, that's him. Here he comes again! Wait! You wake up and realize that you are repeating the ugly incident in the comfort of your own bed. It was all a dream. It's more like a nightmare, but the challenge remains: don't bring that same frustrating, angry, or defeated feeling back to work with you the next day. Most teachers try not to take it home with them, but who are we kidding? We are only human so it can take some time to get over a traumatic experience, especially if your feelings were hurt.

Teachers who deal with niggas will have to try to get used to nasty and ugly incidents. Hopefully they will be based mostly on verbal assaults, but it is a good idea to try to start off each day with a fresh perspective, especially when the culprit has not been suspended or disciplined for cursing you out. I have had niggas who disrespected me and then the next day I acted like nothing ever happened. Teachers cannot afford to hold grudges, or better yet, needy students can't afford us to. We can never truly know all the crap that some students have to put up with throughout the evening and night before they come back to us.

Try to look at every day as a new chance to break the

cycle of ignorance. Continue to smile and show them that you are *Teflon Don* or *Teflon Donna*. Even if you are an amateur, start to work your craft like you have been doing this your whole life. Obviously, if you work with students who have been diagnosed with emotional disabilities, you will have to have the utmost levels of patience and consistency. Rules should be enforced when things get too ugly, but after the dust settles, show them that you are an expert at following Tip One.

**Tip Six - Don't Say The Word!**

Keep it real. *Real* for you as a teacher means being professional. That includes the substitute teachers, too. *Professional* here means that you are getting paid. It also means that you are held to a higher standard of excellence in terms of what you do and what you say. Certified teachers have spent years studying and should know that words are super powerful. Words can build, maintain, or destroy.

No matter the race of teacher, using the word "nigga" or any form of it will not work positively for you. Black teachers do not have a permission slip to use the word in the workplace. Using it as a black man or woman might make you feel cool or that you can relate to students, but in the end, you will be viewed as being unprofessional, unqualified, and ineffective. White teachers and people of other races should especially avoid using the term for both professional and personal reasons. A white teacher may think it is cool or hip to use the term with students who accept it as a term of endearment, but he or she runs the risk of being considered as a racist who is insensitive to the history of the word and race relations. I feel bad for the white teachers who have to hear the term all day, but maintain your integrity, you can relieve the tension of discomfort later on after school with the other 16 hours in your day. Using the word in the classroom or school will only result in the conclusion that you as a teacher are part of the problem and not the solution.

Hang in there white teachers! You know it's a double standard. I can't actually say I know how it feels to be so uncomfortable as you have been, constantly hear a word you can't repeat. When you shout, "Language!" to admonish a student who is speaking inappropriately and that same student responds by asking you, "What did I say?" Crap, you can't even repeat back what they said to identify how inappropriate it was and is. You are handcuffed. Move on and try to refocus the student to the desired behavior and the lesson that you have worked so hard to plan and execute. Make your lessons like a train that can be stopped but not derailed. Don't get suckered into using the n-word in any form. They will bury your career under it.

Sometimes, as you are writing a disciplinary referral, principals and deans will want you to write what the offending student has said - verbatim. I recall writing "the student directed profanity at me and walked out of class without permission". My assistant principal at the time responded when I handed the document to her, saying flatly, "No, Mr. Carter. You have to write down exactly what she said." I felt uncomfortable writing profanities on a piece of paper in my own handwriting. I didn't want a paper trail of my handwriting exposing such vile language, but I did it. I had to. In the case of having to relate an incident in which a student uses the n-word, it's probably better to write just that: *n-word*. I'm sure that should be sufficient. Some of us don't want to have *nigga* on our conscience. Remember Mark Fuhrman.

**Tip Seven - Be Prepared**
Your lessons are a train and the niggas are Jesse James and his gang. Don't let them stop the train or steal the show. They might slow it down, but don't let them stop it! Keep it going even if you have to discipline one or a few. After days, weeks, and semesters, they will see that you mean business. Some of them will cut your class, to avoid riding the unstoppable train. But let them know when they come back that the train is still moving and the fare remains the same: their efforts towards mastery.

Having a lesson plan is a constant reminder even if you never have to look at it during the school day. How much time you spend on planning is determined by your own circumstances, but make a genuine effort to be ready. I never really cared much for recycled lesson plans. With the exception of math teachers, most lesson plans should be customized each school year. You don't want to become mundane or too set in your ways. The students and their interests change and so should you. No one wants to use dated material (even though we all have to), but do the best you can to spice up something considered boring because niggas love to be hip and up-to-date on trends.

Working with niggas without a lesson plan is a contingency for disaster. I have only done it once or twice throughout my career. I can still recall the idea of greeting them at the door with the question in my mind of "OK, what are we going to learn today?" It was not a good feeling. It opens the door for misbehavior because engaging the students in meaningful activities is important for control and classroom management. Those two times I performed spontaneously and managed to pull it off with some production, but I could and would never consider making a habit out of pulling rabbits out of hats in the classroom. A good lesson plan is the backbone necessary to consistently create an environment of learning on a daily basis.

### Tip Eight - Be Vigilant

Be a good listener, but also be very observant. This should be common sense, but you definitely do not want to be behind your desk all day. I made that mistake once. It occurred early in my career during a final exam in a Spanish class. (For the first few years before having my Spanish language certification, I taught Spanish as the one class not endorsed by my Special Education certification. Now, I am certified in both Spanish and Special Education.) I passed out the exams and proceeded to sit behind my desk. I can't remember what I did there besides keep my eyes on the test takers, but when it was over, I found some interesting surprises. There were about three cheat sheets left behind in the desks and chairs.

I had been duped. I was upset at first and then amused. In

the end, I decided not to make the same mistake twice. Since then, I am a floater. I move around so much that it's like I have ADHD (Attention Deficit Hyperactivity Disorder). I can't stay in one place. Sometimes, I am perched on an unoccupied desk or table (even though I encourage students to avoid this). This is the best way to see what is going on and to prevent things that you don't want to happen.

If you can, set up your classroom so that there is no "back of the class". You will start to notice that unless you implement assigned seats, certain students will gravitate towards the areas furthest from you and other students. Sometimes sitting in the back of the class is a part of a defense mechanism on the part of students. One thing that stuck in my mind after reading *The Autobiography of Malcolm X* was that during his last days and times, Malcolm always sat with his back to the wall and his front facing the entrance, especially in restaurants. He would be able to see any obvious threats that might come from the entrance and be able to defend himself. Remember, niggas are not dumb or stupid. Some choose their seating in a classroom to be able to see what's coming while others simply want to sit where they will be ignored or least likely to be called upon.

In my classroom, at the beginning of the semester, I give my students two options: (1) They can have assigned seats; or (2) they can sit wherever they want and give me the power to move them when I feel like it. I have yet to see a class vote for assigned seats when given this option. Niggas will push the envelope and as mentioned before, many have problems respecting authority, but almost everyone agrees that giving your word is a binding contract. An old school hip hop phrase was "word is bond". Remind them of that and how keeping your word is a universal concept in all phases of their lives.

Finally, vigilance can't be effective if you cannot walk around all of your students. Before we had a *zero tolerance* policy on drugs and weapons in my school (pre-Columbine), I confiscated two knives. Since then, I have found vaping devices, permanent markers, porn, cigarettes, and lighters. Of course, cellphones are very disruptive to the educational process and if your school does not have a strict policy that is enforced you will be spending all day policing electronic devices. Set your room up so that you will be able to walk around students to monitor their progress and to keep your classroom safe and orderly. Make sure you verbally engage each student during each class to let them know you acknowledge their presence and their importance to you. Make them feel welcome even though you are simultaneously multitasking to make sure niggas are not up to no good.

I almost lost my job one day when I was being vigilant because I didn't follow through with proper procedure. A female student had her pocketbook on her desk and it was full of items that she was pulling out, placing on the desk. I guessed she was organizing things, maybe looking for a writing utensil. I was walking by her station when I spied a box cutter. Without causing a ruckus, I smoothly and swiftly picked it up and put it in my pocket. If you've ever played jacks, you know how to pick something up without disturbing the surrounding items. After about 3 seconds, she realized what I had done and what I had picked up.

"Give me my stuff back!" she shouted. She didn't say knife, or box cutter, or blade. She said "stuff". I looked at her like I didn't know what she was talking about and she repeated, even louder, "Give me my stuff back!" I walked back to where she was, looked at her and said, "You know you can get in trouble for this, right?"

"Give me my stuff back!" she repeated, one last time. I stood there, and shook my head, "Naw, I can't do that", was my response. I folded my arms. The box cutter was safely in my pocket. None of the other students had seen the potentially deadly tool and now they were looking at me and her, wondering what we were dealing with.

"I need it to be able to walk home from school."

That struck a different type of note in me. I had been where she was, so to say, in life. I had taken a knife to the playground once, a pocket knife, when I got tired of an older kid constantly bullying me day after day. When the older kid came at me one day with the knife in my pocket, I had taken it out, flipped out its sharpest blade, and that's as far as I got with it because my knees began to shake. Up to that moment, I hadn't realized how much heart it took to actually stab someone. That day it ended with him surprised, but unafraid when he said, "Oh! So you gonna stab me?" He saw my fear, mugged me (he pushed me backwards with his hand on my face and forehead), and laughed. I stood there for a moment before going over to sit on a bench where I cried. I went home after a while, but the older kid left me alone after that.

"Please, Mr. Carter. Can I have it back?" she begged. Her shouting had toned down and I could see in her eyes that she felt that she really needed the box cutter to slice her way home if necessary.

"I'll give it back to you after school", was my response. The class continued that period, the lesson was uninterrupted and those students left. During my lunch period, I checked out the box cutter. It was the thumb action type, worked smoothly, and had a brand new blade inside. I removed the blade and reassembled the cutter. Like clockwork, after the final bell, the student showed up and I gave her the blade-less boxcutter. I thought that was the end of it. I figured it wasn't like it had been a gun with no bullets, because a nigga could rob a store with an empty gun, but you won't even get a bag of chips with an empty box cutter.

The next day, I got called into the principal's office. "Did you give a box cutter back to so-and-so?" was the question I faced. I replied that I did, but that I had removed the blade. As a matter of fact, the blade was still in my car and I was willing to retrieve it if necessary. I was given a super stern warning for not immediately turning in the student and my career was still in effect.

From that moment on, I have been in *zero tolerance* mode, no matter who is involved or what my personal feelings are about the situation. The moral of this story continues to be: be vigilant and be prepared to follow up on what you find without prejudice especially if what you find are weapons or drugs. Your career is precious and it should not be lost due to inconsistency in following protocol.

**Tip Nine - Take the Moral High Ground**

To conclude, do what you have to do within your powers as a teacher. I have seen and read so many articles recently of teachers who have had to deal with unruly students on a daily basis with little to no support from administrators. Niggas will push your buttons. They will take your patience to the limit. Unfortunately, when it comes to physical and violent confrontations, self-defense is not always the best option. One of my fellow colleagues was terminated not too long ago simply for defending himself. Several teachers wrote letters stating that he was defending himself and was not striking back as he was attacked by a female student. I was always taught not to hit females, but I am told that this particular student was no lithe and weak girl. When he finally couldn't sustain any more blows from the girl, the former teacher restrained her in a headlock and that's when someone decided to snap a pic. It's a travesty of justice that he would still have his job if he would have let that nigga beat his ass without resisting.

I recently had a student who was not in my class confront me and challenge me to a fight. I was covering a class for an absent teacher. Lately, it's been difficult to get substitutes to sign on to work in school so teachers cover classes during our prep periods for teachers who are out on sick or mental health days. We get a little extra money each time we do it, but it's usually not worth it. It definitely was not worth it that day as I sat in a chair with my back to the door in a room with several students, some of whom were quite unruly.

This particular room had double doors. After a few minutes, I heard the doors open slightly behind me. Pap! A student hit me in the back of the head with a balled up piece of paper. I am bald, so that's the sound it made. I heard two voices laughing and as I opened the doors all the way they ran away. I gave chase, but since the class I was covering was in a remote part of the building, they were long gone. I went back to the room and I was in no mood to be my usual nice self. This time, I sat parallel to the doors and calmly waited and coaxed the slowing of my heartbeat. Not even five minutes had gone by when I heard new movement outside the classroom doors. I heard the movement of scraping against the floor and pictured the paper throwers attempting to barricade the door. I crept towards the door and when I felt the moment was right I pushed it to avoid getting trapped in there along with the other students in the room. A few of the  faces and names were familiar while most of the others were not. They seemed to not notice my little drama, as they lounged around, listening to music, talking loudly, or playing with their cell phones. (The absent teacher hadn't left a substitute lesson plan.)

When I pushed the door, the hall walking paper thrower got bumped by it. The chair that he was trying to wedge under the knob was thrown to the side, and once again, he and his accomplice ran away, laughing. I didn't find anything funny. As a matter of fact, I started to feel like a caged lion who was trapped in a corner with no other way out. I felt that I didn't deserve to be treated and disrespected. I definitely didn't deserve to be hit in the back of my bald head by any objects, whether lethal or not, especially thrown on purpose. I called for security on my cell phone. No one picked up so I called my favorite assistant principal. I told him what happened and asked that he send someone down to deal with the youngster even though I hadn't gotten a good look at him. I didn't even feel like sitting down, but I hoped that the horseplay was over and that I could suffer through this waste of my time in peace. I hoped to check my emails, chit chat with a sensible student, or simply play a couple rounds of gin rummy on my cell phone. I was wrong.

Less than five minutes later, the student came back. Boldly enough, he came back alone. He had fire in his eyes. He opened the door (that did not lock on its own when closed like most of our school's doors), stood there for a second and shouted, "You hit me with the door, motherfucker!" I just looked at him with wide eyes and a look of wonder on my face. "And now we gotta fight!" He didn't say, "And now I'm gonna fuck you up" or "And now I'm gonna beat your ass", he actually said And now we gotta fight.

He started taking off his coat. A thousand thoughts went through my mind in that split second and then my brain focused on two of them: fight him or don't fight him. Even though so many thoughts ran through my mind, none of them seemed to be: you can end your career right here and now. He was smaller, shorter, and weighed less than me. I didn't fear him, but in my thoughts I felt that this would be the moment when I would have to physically defend my life. I was backed into a proverbial corner and there would be nobody to break this one up. Why did this kid choose me today? Why had I become his mark in those moments before he decided to hit me in the head? Who had been raising this kid?

I chose option number two. I stood there, staring at him. I didn't say a word. If a fight or a death was to occur that day it was not going to be due to me taking a swing at a kid before he did the same to me. His coat was off. The fire in his eyes did not die, but he ended the confrontation with words that stung. "You a bitch ass nigga!" He backed off a bit and I reached forward and closed and held the door. With my other hand, unsteady as it was, I called again for security.

I always told myself that when I no longer felt that I could physically defend myself I didn't need to be a teacher anymore. That kid had called me a bitch. Those were fighting words in my neighborhood growing up. I have never been to jail, but I've watched enough TV to know that that word will either get you killed, raped, or sentenced to more time. And there I was, holding the door, waiting for security to come, inevitably feeling like a bitch. Do I have to be a bitch to do this job? I tried to console myself, telling myself that there are no bitches walking along the narrow path of the moral high ground. The narrow path is the most difficult, the most tedious, and the most challenging.

Teaching can be an unfair job. We are more important to the world than professional athletes yet the pay we receive is peanuts compared to what the pros make. We have to take crap from disrespectful young people and come back the next day with smiles on our faces and love in our hearts. Teaching is a difficult job. Teachin' niggas is an even more difficult means of employment. Keep walking that walk and talking your talk. Do it even if it means temporarily compromising your dignity. At the end of each day, you will be able to sleep well knowing that you did the right thing and kept your composure. Do not lose your head even if all those around you lose theirs.

# XVII. AM I A NIGGA, TOO?

*I'm a nigga, he's a nigga, she's a nigga, we some niggaz*
*Wouldn't you like to be a nigga, too?*
*To all my kike niggaz, spic niggaz, guinea niggaz, chink niggaz*
*That's right, y'all my niggaz, too*
*I'm a nigga, he's a nigga, she's a nigga, we some niggaz*
*Wouldn't you like to be a nigga, too*
*They like to strangle niggaz, blaming niggaz, shootin'*
*niggaz, hangin' niggaz*
*Still you wanna be a nigga, too? True..*

- Nas "Be A Nigger Too"

I remember an incident that happened in one of my earliest years of teaching. There were three students in my class who refused to begin the assignment after about ten minutes of me trying to convince them to do so. Two of them were black twelfth graders, and one was a Puerto Rican eleventh-grader. I said to them, "Look guys, if you're not going to get to work, I am going to have to ask you to leave. You are making it impossible for the other students to learn." I was hoping that that would be enough prodding to get them to at least give me a half-effort. The two twelfth-graders surprised me by walking out of the room. I looked at the eleventh-grader and after a second or two, he followed the others out of the door. I went on with the rest of the class and wrote referrals for the slackers.

The next day when the 11th grader was the first to show up, I handed him his referral at the door and told him to take that to the principal. I turned around and walked back into the room to get class started. It was then that I heard the 11th grader in the hallway talking in a loud voice to a roaming student, shouting, "Man, fuck that nigga!" I heard him repeat it again after that, "Man, fuck that nigga!"

I practically ran to the door and into the hallway. My heart was pumping with adrenaline as I shouted down the corridor to the 11th grader, "Yo! What 'chu say?!"

He looked back at me and did not reply, but I wasn't finished. "Here I am! Come and do it! Come "f" me up!" (Despite how mad I was, I *still* didn't curse. I said the letter *f*.)

The 11th grader kept walking, but turned to look back. He said, "Man, Go 'head."

I'm sure that there was fire in my eyes as the blood of the streets pumped through my veins, but I knew a retreat when I saw one, and a retreat is exactly what the 11th grader had accomplished. And just like when the niggas who I had grown up with on the streets had the upper hand, played that hand, and won, I had to put the dominating icing on the cake. "Oh, that's what I thought!", I shouted, for all those in the classroom and in the halls to hear. Getting the last word for a nigga is like getting in the last punch in a one-on-one street fight. The crowd almost always remembers the fighter who got in the last punch as the winner.

It was like the time I got jumped by three guys in the park, back when we were kids. I was maybe 12 or 13 years old. I don't even remember why the fight started or why I was the target of the three other guys. Two of them were my age and one was younger. I do remember punching two of them and they stopped jumping me, leaving me to fight one-on-one with a kid that I'll call "Rock". Rock and I boxed for a little while with the other two looking on. Slowly but surely, a crowd started to form. Rock never got any real hits in on me and I never got any major shots in on him either, but I do recall he held my sleeves for most of the end of the fight as I struggled to get loose from him and punish him for the entire fiasco. I wasn't a brawler, but my dad always taught me to defend myself.

It felt like the fight went on forever, but it probably lasted about 10 minutes. At the end, we were surrounded by a crowd of people and there were some older kids who tried to break us up. One kid tried to hand Rock a bat so he could take a real swing at me, (ironically, it was my bat!), but fortunately for me, there was someone in the crowd who didn't want me to get my brains bashed in and my little league wooden baseball bat never made it into Rock's hands.

As the older kids finally got us apart and ended the fight, Rock jumped over someone and took a swing at me. His punch landed square on my cheek. It made a loud smacking sound because I had my mouth open, panting from the long, arduous struggle that winded me. Several people in the crowd shouted "Ooo-ooh!" and the chorus of their voices resounded in unison, giving it a harmony of sorts. Even though the punch didn't hurt, it meant a lot to the crowd, to Rock, and to me. He had gotten the last punch. After all that time he spent holding me, and even though I had successfully defended myself against three guys all by myself, the crowd saw him get the last punch. Rock had played his hand and won.

Do I have some nigga in me?

It took me a couple of minutes to calm down after that incident in the classroom and hallway. The students in class helped me out by not making matters worse. I did push-ups in class to use up that adrenaline that still had me hyped up. We eventually laughed it off, and those students wound up performing well in class that year, but they had succeeded in taking me out of character.

Is there a nigga teaching my class?

I thought back to how I was. Standing in the middle of the hallway, in full and clear view of the high-definition surveillance cameras, requesting physical violence from a minor. Isn't that what niggas do? When their buttons are pressed, aren't they capable of losing it all for a little bit of street credentials?

Is there a nigga cashing my paycheck?

When pushed to the limit, almost any teacher will snap, right? I've been there before, but I've never truly been physically assaulted by a student. I am not a really big guy (6", 190 lbs), but

I have found myself stating that I am capable of turning self-defense into offense. (Oh wow! That is almost identical to a lyric from the hip-hop group Cypress Hill!). Is that just the street in me or a true defense mechanism that goes along with the environment? But I know that I won't be young and strong forever, so I almost always try to rely more on my wit and crafty language to avoid potentially dangerous conflicts.

I've almost always been able to shake off any anger quickly, focusing on the lesson after the culprit is removed, refocuses or decides to get to work too. When teachin' niggas, the lesson plan is like a train that will make many stops, but will reach the destination if the conductor is focused. That's how I feel about myself. I try not to let the train go off the track or get delayed for too long at a particular stop. However, sometimes, it is inevitable.

Many a day, my first period class trickles in and then they want to talk about a shooting or a death that happened the night before. My job becomes one of a counselor, social worker, or psychologist. I am no expert, but you do not need multiple degrees to become a good listener. I encourage dialogue that is respectful. If I can accomplish that in moments of crisis, the planned lesson can wait. But still there are times when the conversation is foolish and obviously a waste of the precious time that we have to learn and expand young minds. A nigga solves many problems with violence or the threat of violent action. It's a part of the bravado that legitimizes niggas in the eyes of other niggas. It's not a good teacher tactic to challenge a student with potential violence because sooner or later there will be a student who is ready, willing, and able to call my bluff.

The question is still there: Is my wife's husband a nigga?

Over the years, I have talked to a lot of men who would not last one hour on my job or in my position. High school girls are too much of a temptation for a nigga. I guess that is why teaching is a female-dominated profession for the most part in this country. Not to say that women aren't hot for young blood, (there are former female teachers behind bars right now for having sex with young male students), but male niggas are trained to conquer women sexually. Hip hop culture dictates sexual conquest. As soon as they find out where I work, I have seen guy's eyes light up and say something like, "Man, if I was teachin' over there, I would have this one, that one, *and* have that one for dinner!" I usually laugh and let them know that they wouldn't make it to their first payday thinking like that.

I was helping out on a home improvement job (I like to work construction jobs during the summer because it's physical labor, involves no homework and the pay is cold hard cash) and one of the workers who is pushing forty stops working every five to ten minutes when a young girl walked by. He would make lewd and crude sexual comments about what he would do to them and all I could do was smile. What could I say? Why stress myself out by trying to rehabilitate a pervert? When one girl waved to me and I waved back, he almost lost his breath asking me who she was. I told him in a matter-of-fact way, "Oh, she was in my second period class." He took even more time off of the task at hand to tell me that based on her physical appearance, he couldn't believe that she was a high school student. It didn't even seem to make him feel guilty when I told him that she probably wasn't even 16-years old.

I am no eunuch, but if I am checking out anyone at work, it's the female staff members and the cafeteria ladies. Adults. Even though the age of consent is sixteen in my state, it is still morally wrong to troll for young tail as a teacher. It is also a violation of school district policies. When I look at female students, it's not in a sexual way. I think of my own daughters. To me, it's sick to look upon a young girl with lust if she is underage or younger than my own offspring. There's no Catholic priest or R Kelly lurking inside of me. Even though no one can convict me for my thoughts, my conscious is clear.

What gets a nigga in trouble is his mouth and hands that convict him or her. Lately, girls wear pants and shirts that show the crack in their butts, especially when they are sitting down. Stretch pants, yoga pants, and tights are also inappropriate for any professional setting. There will always be cleavage too, from here until eternity. I had a student who wore very high mini skirts and shirts that exhibit her cleavage (double jeopardy). She gets away with it with security and administration and enjoys flaunting herself as far as I can tell. A nigga will say something because that's what niggas do. Niggas have no filter. Seeing a butt crack or deep cleavage is a trigger for him *(or her)* to shoot off at the mouth with something seductive that school district administrations would term "sexual harassment".

One of our principals said that he would balk at reprimanding a female student for exposing her butt crack because the response could be, "Why are you looking?" So, it's basically a trap. I can feel when the wind is hitting me in the butt, so those girls and women have to be able to as well. I avoid hugging female students too, because I wouldn't want a male teacher hugging one of my daughters. Hugs can turn into much more. A fist bump or a high five are the safest and best ways for me to greet someone with physical contact.

Is there a nigga downloading songs onto my computer?

Opening up my music folder on my computer will reveal many folders, but one is labeled "Hip Hop". Inside of that folder are some tunes that I definitely would not want my children to listen to. These are songs I might listen to in my car while driving alone, or through headphones. There are some songs in that folder that I am ashamed to say that I like. There are songs in that folder that will make me look like a hypocrite. Hip hop music presents an inner conflict for me.

There's gangsta rap and more rap that is laced with profanity in my folder. It's stuff that my students would consider to be "old". Trap music is not for me. The rap music of the 2010's doesn't really appeal to me. I guess it's the flow, the so-called *mumble rap* that sounds to me like the artist is laying in bed, rhyming some tired, shallow lyrics about selling drugs, having sex, and the usual materialism. I don't care that I haven't kept up with the new trends. I have matured enough to enjoy what I like even though the modern crowd has left me behind in the 2000's, '90's and even the '80's. Maybe I'm out of touch with contemporary hip hop, but if the core message is still materialism, sex, drugs, and violence, then I pretty much get the picture.

I have the most thugged-out hits in a folder called "Hard Core". 1999's hit "More Money, More Cash, More Hoes", by Jay-Z is one of the songs that comes to mind. It might be "old" to you, but I'm probably old to you, too. It raps about drug dealing, making money, spending money, violence and sex. Of course, the word *nigga* makes its regular and frequent cameo appearances in the lyrics. Why? "Just 'cause I love my niggas!" Why do I listen to this song through headphones? It has to be that beat; that base-line that will have me humming it from the back of my throat for hours after hearing the track. I even have the instrumental. Boom, boom, boom-boom-boom! I love Digable Planets and Cypress Hill. I like Tupac and the R&B group 112. They all use the word *nigga* to varying degrees.

In Spanish, I really get down with reggaeton from the *playero* era: the 2000's. Reggaeton is like the Puerto Rican version of hip hop, in my opinion. It is also worldwide, with artists hailing from other Latin American countries. I listen to the overly sexualized music of Julio Voltio, Tego Calderón, and my all time favorites *Jowell y Randy*. Once again, my native language students will say that I listen to old music in Spanish, but even though Voltio's music from ten years ago is sexually charged (his song *Dáme D'eso* means "Give Me That" and now he is a Gospel preacher), his music was not so blatant and pornografic as reggaeton has become in the 20-teens.

I have written my own raps, but none of them have the word *nigga* in them. Maybe that's why I never became a commercial rapper. The industry would have put my Will Smith-styled rap right up on the shelf, with a puff of dust coming from them tossing it up there for emphasis.

Am I a nigga?

I still refuse to be called a nigga or a nigger. (If I can help it.) I do not use the word in my spoken language. I know that you find that hard to believe after counting how many times the word appears in this writing, but you can ask people who know me, including students and former students. They have been around me and have heard me talk more than anyone. I am trying to teach them to avoid degrading themselves with the term. As I learned in behavior modification class, I model the desired behavior.

Still today, niggas will come up to me and say, "What's up, my nigg?!?" Or they will use the expression, "My nigga!", that Denzel Washington made popular in his Oscar award performance in the movie *Training Day*. If it's a student who greets me that way, I have a few pre-recorded responses. I say, "I'm a black man". I sometimes stray from that and respond with "I'm nobody's nigg", but I usually go with the "black man" statement to avoid having to use the term myself and to reinforce the idea to me that there is a difference between a black man and a nigga. If the person who greets me is a peer or someone older, I simply acquiesce, slump my shoulders, smile, and say, "What's up?!"

Once upon a time, I would send a student to the principal's office for using the word "nigga". I would write on the referral that the student used profanity and racial slurs. At first, I didn't think I was wasting my time. I wanted the message to get across that there is a time and place for all types of language. The classroom is not a place for vile talk. I also want them to know that they need to prepare for life after high school. Niggas can and will get fired for using the n-word on the job. I don't want them to look back after getting canned and say, "Well, my teacher used to call us that and he said it was OK." I simply don't endorse its use. I want them to think back on me and other teachers who kept it real and remember that we tried to prepare them for success and tried to give them the ability to control one of the most powerful weapons people can wield - the tongue.

# XVIII. THE FUTURE

*We gotta make a change*
*It's time for us as a people to start makin' some changes.*
*Let's change the way we eat, let's change the way we live*
*And let's change the way we treat each other.*
*You see, the old way wasn't working so it's on us to do*
*What we gotta do, to survive.*

- Tupac Shakur "Changes"

As soon as you read the title, you probably asked your-self, "Can people who consider themselves niggas be taught?" The whole concept of *niggardom* (a term used by comedian Katt Williams) is an idea of ignorance. Teachers and administrators will continue to try. It is still an honorable and noble job. It's a hard, frustrating job, too. In some states, schools will close due to their poor academic performance, especially if their viability is determined by standardized testing. Society is trying to come to terms with post-secondary niggas by providing social welfare programs, low-skilled labor opportunities, and building more prisons. However, the world is heading in a different direction. Technology has improved and increased to the level where un-skilled workers can expect slim pickings.

The eight years of having a black, African American president have come and gone. Barack Obama was everything that the race men and women of color dreamed about: an articulate, intelligent, trustworthy black man who rose up through the ranks and became the first black president of the United States of America. (Twice!) With his beautiful wife and daughters by his side, he was not perfect, but he helped to create a sense of pride within the

African American community and helped to show the world that not all black people consider themselves *niggas*.

Has the word and the use of the word *nigga* disappeared after having a black president? No, unfortunately, it has not. Barack Obama used the word *nigger* once in a public forum to discuss and explain how racism has not disappeared and that it is still a part of the American psyche. However, I wanted our first black president to address *nigga*, and how the youth of our society has manipulated a racist word and turned it into what they consider a term of endearment. I wanted our first black president to flip the script on those youngsters and plant a seed in their minds that teachers like myself and others could cultivate through instruction to enhance the annihilation of ignorance.

I do hope that the practice of calling each other "nigga" will be a trend that dies out. I too have a dream. Thanks, Dr. Martin Luther King, Jr. I hope that all of the people who are appalled by the use of the term in this writing will be angry and motivated enough to come up with a way to end the *nigga era*. I wish that those of you who criticize my surrender to the nigga idea will be so perturbed that you educate your children and provide them with activities that will help them grow into productive citizens. I feel your disgust. I have spent many moments fighting the notion of "please don't use that term".

The difference between the critics and I is that I have literally, figuratively, and academically fought against the use of the term. I have been in the trenches for so long that I have forgotten some names while remembering faces. I continue to fight and struggle to this day. My frustration and feelings of pessimism have not caused me to stop the routine of warfare. I still say "thanks" or "gracias" when a student asks me to excuse him or her for using the term in my presence. When that happens, I consider it an accomplishment. I continue to inform them that the term is unprofessional. Unless they want to lose points in writing assignments, they must edit by replacing the word with something more descriptive.

But in my heart, I see the trend as being vibrant and strong.

The war in the classroom is a seven and a half hour battle. Ignorance is an evil revolutionary vanguard that attempts to win, disrupt, recruit or to simply exist. Good teachers, good students, upwardly mobile parents, and administrators are the established regime that want the status quo to be successful and establish achievement as the norm, cultivating it in power and growth. Niggas are education's insurgents. They can be the psychological terrorists of the academic world. When those rebels succeed in disrupting the classrooms on a regular basis, it begins to affect the entire school's performance. It can get to be so overwhelming, especially in low-income, urban areas.

There have been times in my career when some adults, administrators and teachers approached me to pass a student who was legitimately failing my class. This was after numerous attempts to assist, modify my instruction, differentiate my techniques, and contact parents and guardians for assistance. I have always had the idea that I don't actually *fail them*, they pass or fail *themselves*. I hope that I haven't been perceived to be obnoxious when I've corrected teachers who would say something like "I failed 'so-in-so' in my Biology class. She just didn't attempt to do the work." I would always counter by saying, "No, she failed *herself*."

One particular student for which administration encouraged me to provide a passing grade was a young man who fit most of the nigga criteria, but he was also a nice guy who had a great sense of humor. I was requested to pass him because "failing him will do him no good". I'm sorry. I am very empathetic, but I was raised and taught to tell the truth. I equate teachers that pass students who legitimately fail with dirty cops. Taking a bribe or stealing a stash is just as bad as falsifying a grade. Once you go dirty, you can never truly be clean again.

Even though I felt sorry for him and his home situation, that could not justify me giving him something that he didn't deserve. It's not like I didn't make and provide many opportunities for him to make up work, do extra work, or reintroduce the lesson when he would arrive to class 30 minutes late. That's another big challenge with teachin' niggas. We, as teachers, are under pressure to conform to standards and at the same time we are under pressure to accommodate for substandard students. If I sink and fall to a level of sub-standardized teaching, I would be digging a hole that is inescapable. It's different when a student has an IEP (Individualized Educational Plan) and is learning disabled. The IEP dictates specific goals and sometimes those students will not achieve all of my class goals and objectives, nor will they be able to complete each and every assignment. That's a different ballgame. Notwithstanding, I would much rather go on record in the students' memories that I had integrity. The student who I was requested to pass did fail and eventually went to summer school for my subject, but afterwards he respected me and I knew that I did the right thing.

I don't hate niggas. I don't like some of them, but there are many who are lovable and enjoyable to be around. There are some niggas who can still be considered "nice kids". Many times, they are caught up into the streets or their parents do not invest the time and effort into raising them with love and instruction. Sometimes, a nigga might need 10-15 minutes to let off some of the steam and frustration from their daily lives to be able to learn. Unfortunately, those precious minutes add up and in the end, the lost time only compounds their problems in the present and future. Niggas can be under so much pressure because of the lifestyles they have chosen or due to the outside influences on their lives that they cannot control. However, out of all this negative drama a young person can emerge - genuine at heart and capable of rising above their obstacles.

I have had niggas in my class who have turned out to be model citizens. I feel good when some of them come up to me a few years or more after graduating and let me know that my work was not in vain. It seems like they respect me for "keeping it real", not wasting their time, not giving them free time in class, and always having a lesson prepared. They seem to show a lot less respect for teachers who treated them like niggas and didn't care enough about them to talk to them or get to know them.

I recently saw a student who used to fit the nigga criteria while enrolled in my class during high school. Now, he has a job, a new car, an apartment, and stability. When we shook hands at the gas station, he smiled and said, "Mr. Carter, now I see what you were talking about!" He finally understood that life is about working, paying bills, being responsible, and avoiding pitfalls. That made me feel good and I told him that I was proud of him. I was genuine and truthful with him. As he told me about the things he legitimately has accomplished, I thought about how other people might think that he was bragging. But to a good teacher, he was just displaying comprehension of what he had retained and was excited about giving me a verbal presentation in list form.

Being a nigga does not have to be a permanent condition. "Nigga" and "nigger" denote ignorance, no matter the idea that some niggas seem to think they know it all. It does take a strong will and desire for a nigga to overcome and become someone with self-esteem, respect, and a career. To be a part of that conversion is what many teachers and students today can strive for, work towards, and live for. Teaching is a lifestyle that does not end when the bell rings. We take it home with us. We sleep with it. We think about new ideas and different methods to utilize in the classroom everywhere: from being stuck in a traffic jam, while out on a vape break, to sitting on the toilet.

My father was a preacher. Even though I didn't want to grow up to be a minister or pastor like him, in some ways I envied his ability to humbly say that he led someone to accept the Lord Jesus Christ. To a Christian, that is the ultimate chest-pounding victory. Even for a humble person, to be able to lead someone out of darkness is deserving of a sense of pride. When I see a former student like the one at the gas station who was a pure-bred nigga in school, but who is now a legitimate man with a bright future, my frustration disappears. I feel worthy of my calling. My work is not in vain. It actually feels even better to see a converted nigga become a productive and successful man or a woman than it does to meet up with the good students later on in their lives.

So, there is hope. Tomorrow's lesson is already planned. The weekend is over and again it is time to offer water to those who will drink. I wonder what the conversation will center on as they trickle into the classroom in the morning. What happened in the community this weekend that I will have to manipulate into a learning experience? As much as I despise the nigga attitudes, I look forward to seeing the students. They frustrate me with their nigga ways, but I have much love for them. Will the word ever be truly laid to rest in our communities? Only time will tell, because the leaders of our society have failed to kill the word. Some of our leaders have reinforced its use by alienating themselves from certain sectors in society.

In thinking about school tomorrow, who will be the first to use the despised word? Who will remind me of the self-image that our young people continue to promote? Who will give me *nigga* for breakfast?

# BIOGRAPHY

**Wesley D. Carter** is a former recipient of the U.S. Army Reserve's Scholar Athlete Award. As an Urban Studies major who graduated from the University of Pennsylvania, he went on to serve his country as a U.S. Peace Corps Volunteer in Guatemala, Central America. Wanting to make a direct and positive impact on his community, Wesley returned to the United States and became the first Bilingual Special Education teacher in an urban school district in southeastern Pennsylvania. Since completing his post-graduate studies at Cheyney University and Temple University, Mr. Carter has been a Special Education and Spanish teacher for more than 25 years and also is a Certified Educator for Duolingo. Besides his service promoting organic pesticides and fertilizers in rural Guatemala, Wesley has traveled to El Salvador, Cuba, and the Dominican Republic. Currently he resides in New Jersey with his wife and daughters where he teaches Spanish and writes.

Made in the USA
Middletown, DE
20 August 2019